C000124674

Dear John:
Letters You'll Never Read

MARCIA BYARS WILLETT

BGB
Bronze Goose Books

Dear John: Letters You'll Never Read

All rights reserved. No part of this book may be reproduced or used in any manner whatsoever without the prior written permission of the copywrite owner, except for the use of brief quotations in reviews.

For more information contact
www.bronzegoosebooks.com

FIRST EDITION published 2023
Copyright © 2023 Marcia Byars Willett

Dear John: Letters You'll Never Read

can be purchased in quantities for book clubs, readings, etc.
For more information email marcia.fpgb@gmail.com

MARCIA BYARS WILLETT

is available for speaking engagements and book discussions.
For more information email marcia.fpgb@gmail.com

Cover image and interior designed by © Danold
Portrait Photo Credit © Karen Bullock

ISBN 979-8-218-95869-5

Bronze Goose Books

PRINTED IN THE UNITED STATES OF AMERICA

© Karen Bullock

About the Author

MARCIA BYARS WILLETT, retired Presbyterian pastor, lives in Theodore, Alabama where she writes, raises critters, and eagerly awaits visits from her four grandchildren. Her work has been published in *Words Have Wings, a Carpe Stylum! Anthology of Poetry and Art* and *Out Of Darkness Came the Word, a Carpe Stylum! Anthology of Short Stories.* Willett chose the written word to walk through her grief when her 36-year relationship with John ended with his death in 2019. Married in 1983, divorced in 2017, and reunited in 2019, just months before his death, Willett dealt with that loss by writing a series of letters to John as if he were able to receive them in the celestial realms. Using frankness and emptying her grief onto the page with raw emotion and brutal honesty, Willett strove to accept the loss of her loved one through letters from the date of his death to its one-year anniversary.

Having traveled in Europe, the next item on Willett's bucket list is to see all the bluest lakes in the United States and Canada.

To my children, Joey and Jordan,
who know this story and the man in a very different way,
but who can appreciate it
for what it is.

Acknowledgements

As I am not, at this point, accepting an Oscar for Best Adaptation of a Memoir, I feel comfortable with thanking as many people as I feel made it possible for Dear John to become a book someone might actually purchase and read. John has been gone for four years, but it would be ungracious not to acknowledge the man who provided such rich fodder for my pen. I really do hope you have a first-rate set of golf clubs, honey. You deserve them.

The first encouragement to publish came from many friends who read these letters and stories when I posted them on Facebook. Thank you all. Without your repeated requests to finally publish the letters, they would have remained unknown outside the realm of social media.

Missy Buchanan, an esteemed advocate and writer of multiple books on aging faithfully and gracefully, graciously provided support as a reader and recommender of publishers who might be interested in publishing Dear John. LuWanda Cheney of Bronze Goose Books has my undying gratitude for officially making an author out of me. Her skill and guidance were invaluable. My thanks to Danold for his amazing attention to detail and for the artistry that will draw the eye to the cover of the book. Carpe' Stylum, the writing group through which I was introduced to LuWanda and Bronze Goose Books gave me reasons to keep writing and to try to

write well. Brenita Mitchell and Laura Foley nudged me to believe I could do this, so I did. Karen Bullock photographed me for the cover and made me look good—no small feat.

Since *Dear John: Letters You'll Never Read* is ultimately a book of love and faith, I thank God heartily for making this journey with me.

—Marcia Byars Willett

Dear John:
Letters You'll Never Read

"Life is pleasant. Death is peaceful. It's the transition that's troublesome."

—Isaac Asimov

Table Of Contents

Foreword

During the summer of 2011, I had traveled to the Mississippi Gulf Coast from my home in North Texas to help Lucimarian, the mother of Good Morning America's Robin Roberts, pen her memoir, *My Story, My Song*. As a writer-speaker on topics of aging faithfully, I had become friends with Lucimarian and was honored to capture her rich life stories on paper. On Sunday mornings during July, I sat beside Lucimarian in her small Presbyterian church in Bay St. Louis as sunlight spilled through the stained glass and onto my lap. I remember thinking how Lucimarian's description of John and Marcia was on point. They were funny, smart, and refreshingly authentic. You could sense that their faith had been honed by traversing the uneven landscape of life.

In April 2012, when Lucimarian's book was released, I reconnected with John and Marcia at a special book launch event across the bridge from Bay St. Louis in Pass Christian. Then only four months later, I sat in their familiar sanctuary once again. This time, it overflowed with grieving family members and friends, and a group of high-profile television celebrities as John and Marcia led the homegoing service following Lucimarian's death.

Since that day in 2012, my admiration and respect for Marcia Willett has only deepened. After John's unexpected death in 2019, Marcia discovered a unique way to deal with her loss and grief: a series of Dear John Letters chock-full of her signature wit and gut-wrenching honesty. Even from across the miles, the letters had me laughing and crying at times, a reminder that grief is a tangled ball of emotions even for the most devoted Christian and that healing often comes with a big dose of humor.

After reading the Dear John letters, I thought about my widowed friends who have expressed disappointment in Christian books on grief that suggest a step-by-step formula to get out of the dark valley. Marcia understands that grief is messy and complicated, with no timeline in sight. She invites you to pull up a chair at her kitchen table and explore your innermost thoughts together. Grab a cup of coffee, get a box of tissues, and take a seat. Let Marcia be the friend who offers you her authentic heart instead of just another cliche'.

—Missy Buchanan, Author and Speaker

Prologue

"Yearning: (n) a tender or urgent longing."

It's hard to know what to say to people who are grieving the loss of someone they love. I don't use the past tense, because the absence of the loved one doesn't eradicate your memories or feelings for them. And you can't marginalize or process those emotions in an afternoon by giving yourself a good talking-to. Nor can you compartmentalize them. If love is complicated, grief is exponentially more complex in terms of how it makes us feel and how we deal with it. Primarily, that's because grief has no real or palpable presence on which to place our burden. There is no broken wedding glass to sweep up or kiss-and-makeup session after an argument—just empty space and an aching heart. Even the most sympathetic shoulder can't assuage the yearning for that missing person, especially if the living and the dead have had a long-standing relationship.

You will not see the word yearning a lot in my letters to John. But as a pastor and believer, I think yearning is what most of us discover we are left with when the flurry of funeral arrangements, memorials, casseroles, sympathy cards, and those dying carnations stop coming. A very good pastor friend of mine once told me that the best way to be when you are with someone who is grieving is to simply cry with them when they are crying and laugh with them when they are laughing. I think this is eloquent if elegiac advice, and I have practiced doing exactly that when loved ones die. But I must admit the temptation to say something profound and comforting can be overwhelming.

A piece of friendly advice: No one, absolutely no one, wants to hear how happy said loved one is now that he or she is with the Lord and that we should celebrate his/her passing.

When God takes a loved one to His home, they are then absent from your home. This is a hard blow. And when things do settle down, and the aloneness settles in—when your husband is gone, your mom is gone, your child is gone—the silence once filled with the sounds of their voices can be a soul killer. God has promised us He will always be with us and that He will never leave us. And that is the truth. But death is a massive blow to those left behind. I can't pretend that I'm not still struggling with John's absence.

Acknowledging the flaws in your relationship is not being disrespectful or callous toward the dead. It's history. It's the history of your life with your loved one. Pretending they were sainted and perfect will only bring you more misery as you work your way into a life without them. It's healthy to remember the good and the bad. Keep your relationship real. Keep both kinds of memories alive. Remembering some of the more despicable moments has kept me sane on days when grief threatened to suffocate me. I am working my way to less regret and more yearning. There won't ever be a day when I don't want to talk to John, including a planned first post-death conversation in which I royally chew him out for not calling me that Sunday for our late-night discussion of our worship services, the dog's behavior, and whether or not we were going to Boston or Denver to see either of our children and grandchildren in the spring. I consider his being dead as no excuse.

I lost John in April of 2019. We had been married for 34 of the 36 years we had known each other. There are those moments when I remember the most pleasant events in our life together and smile. Then there are those moments that come to mind when I simply wanted to hit him over the head with a frying pan. I remember those, too. I find that helpful when I'm assaulted by the yearning for more than a day. I remind myself that John was no saint. He missed countless birthdays and anniversaries. The first word out of his mouth when his children asked him to do something with them was always "No," even if he ended up doing it later. He laid his dirty laundry directly on top of the laundry hamper. And that's just the inconsequential stuff. There were far more substantive issues that complicated our lives and made for some awful periods in our marriage.

As a result, I did a lot of grieving by myself. On days I missed John acutely, I struggled to find an appropriate outlet for a feeling that's similar to having all the air snatched out of your lungs at once. Birthdays and Father's Day were tough for our kids, but I felt awkward calling to comfort them. We were divorced. And John had died alone in the hallway of his apartment, scant weeks after we had decided that a life together was once again possible despite all evidence to the contrary. I voluntarily took on loads and loads of guilt. It was and is the heaviest part of the burden that I bear. That scene flashes before my eyes, my heart drops into my stomach, and I whisper to no one, "Oh, Honey."

If you have lost a loved one, and I don't care if it was yesterday or 15 years ago, I am praying for you, even though I've never met you and probably never will. May your grief find an outlet that will lighten your load just a little bit, and may the yearning become more wistful than gut-wrenching and lonely. I know you may feel like you are alone right now, but you are not. You're not. Claiming your faith at this time might be hard, but don't ever forget, God IS always with you.

Allow yourself to grieve in exactly the way you want, short of doing yourself harm. If you want to lie in bed for three days straight (and your boss won't fire you), do that. I don't suggest you do this every day for a year but eat that quart of ice cream if you want to. Don't let anyone (and I mean ANYONE) shame you about the way you deal with such great loss. If someone says, "Don't you think it's time to move on, dear," give them a good mental smack on the head.

Don't let your friends' attention and attempts to comfort you put you off. That is their way of grieving with you. Turn off your ears and just nod your head occasionally if it's too painful to take part in a real, live conversation.

Oh, and by the way. Grief doesn't necessarily move forward in a regimented march through the passage of time, but the blows won't be as lethal as they were a week ago, a year ago, a decade ago. You have the strength to go on living. If you don't think you do, reach out. Reach out to a professional. Unless they are a mental health professional, no friend, however close, can pull you in from a ledge that is so personal and so dangerous. Joining your loved one in death is not the way to attenuate such a loss. I am giving you serious advice here.

It is okay to share your feelings. Know you are not alone. If you or a loved one is struggling, or just need someone to truly listen, call 988, day or night. Feel supported and connected with trusted people who can help you navigate these waters.
988 Suicide and Crisis Lifeline

Sometime last May, it crossed my mind that I should write some of these feelings down. I was a writer, wasn't I? I should write. My grief was not so precious that it could not be shared. So, I wrote my first Dear John letter. Writers desperately need to be read, so I posted it on Facebook. That way, I felt my struggle was validated. I shared my pain with other friends without having to look them in the eye and try not to cry. I sobbed at John's memorial. My heart declared that one deluge was enough. That I ugly cried in front of a host of other people still makes me squirm just a little bit. My thing about crying is in no way meant to demean those who weep for the one they love. It's just a thing with me. Fodder for a psychiatrist's couch.

Some 20 letters and several vignettes later, many Facebook friends told me that those letters had helped them deal with the grief of a lost loved one in their lives. They told me they found comfort in the fact that they were not alone in the roller coaster intensity and nature of their grieving. I, myself, found writing about John cathartic.

I wrote my feelings down and then basically shared them with the whole world. My dad tells me all the time that a

Facebook post can be seen by any living human being, whether they are your Facebook friend or not. Since grief is a universal experience, I'm good with that. The written word sort of held my hand and made me feel less confounded and angry and so deeply, deeply sad. Writing these letters helped me, one at a time, face unfamiliar and troubling realities about John's loss. Writing, in a very real sense, saved me.

Grief is unique to each griever.

Reading these letters won't alleviate your grief, but they might address some of your struggle to deal with it. They won't cure what ails you, as my grandmother used to say, but they might help, and I hope they make you laugh. It is good to know you are not alone when you have feelings and reactions to memories that don't make sense in the tactile world. People want to deal with things that are tangible, that they can put their hands on. Heck, I want to deal with things that are tangible, that I can put my hands on. But death is not one of those things. John's absence will never be righted by anything I do or say or feel. The intensity of what I feel these days may abate sometime in the future, but I think the yearning will always remain.

I pray you will understand the strength you have in God to bear up under an awful burden. I hope you will find your way out of the pain and learn how to deal with the yearning.

I wish I could alleviate your pain.

But your journey is your own. If these letters ameliorate your suffering even a little bit, then my grief has found some purpose in its expression. Thanks be to God and may God bless you with infinite tender care and mercies all the days of your life.

Letter Number One

Dear John,

Your memorial was today, and love is on my mind. Love that draws my heart even into the vacuum that death creates when it calls a beloved home. A home that is not yet my home. A home that is not here. A home that moves the person I love just out of the reach of my hands that want to touch. To hold onto. To cling to the elbow of the beloved as he turns his face away from earthly loves and toward his Creator. "Go with great blessing!" I know this is what my heart should cry. The words trailing after you to God's kingdom like sheets of music which diminish and fade in bright sunlight. "Wait!" my heart cries out, "We're not through talking. I didn't finish telling you about Juliet's birthday present. You haven't told me about your Sunday. We always talk about our Sundays. Wait! Don't go. Let me hear, 'Alright, kid,' just one more time.' No? You are such a stubborn man. Fine. I'll see you around. I'll miss you so much. Save me a good spot. I love you."

May God grant you peace as He receives you into your eternal home, John Robert Willett. Husband, friend, father, editor, confidante, colleague in ministry, beloved Bear. May 21, 1947 until April 7, 2019.

Letter Number Two

Dear John,

Damn boy, this is hard! In three weeks, I've managed to get one load of laundry done. One. And that was a desperation load because I was running out of underwear. I spent almost two hours trying to separate darks from lights—a 10-minute job at best. I am moving like the blood in my veins is lead. Bob[1] says this is normal. I know that's true. I think he misses you, too.

Let's talk about frozen dinners. I wasted several pounds of meat I couldn't force myself to cook. So, I've been reduced to meatloaf and mashed potatoes from the freezer. I don't even like meatloaf. Although, Boston Market's meatloaf could be worse. Tonight at Greer's, I bought three bags of lima beans. Why? They should last a while. Of course, they're not edible without a little piglet, are they?

---

1   Bob was a psychologist who counseled Marcia and John during their hard times.

I sold some of your stuff. I didn't think I could do that, either, but I did. I used the money to buy a ticket to France. At first, I was giddy. Then, I thought about all the times we talked about going to your beloved Austria. Which is a memory impregnated with irony since you wouldn't even take me to one of your college reunions one whole state away. This made me sad, too. Bob says this is normal. I know that's true.

I couldn't say goodbye to Henri. That I really could not do. I saw him without intending to, and he started wiggling. I turned my back on him, got in your truck, and drove off. Well, you can imagine how that felt. He misses you. I know that's true.

A woman I know lost her husband suddenly several years ago. We were sharing our stories over coffee and doughnuts. She reached across the table and touched my hand. I burst into tears. Which sort of surprised the girls behind the counter. Surprised me, too. Bob would say that this is perfectly normal. While that may be true, it doesn't mean I have to like it. I can't wear waterproof mascara. You know that's true.

Letter Number Three

Dear John,

Today, I picked up the phone three times
to call you and gripe about something. When
I realized I couldn't do that, my heart seized
up just a little and felt smaller in my chest.
I'm pretty much acting like a normal person—
working, writing sermons, preaching, visiting
people, eating lunch with the Huffmans and
the Adams, sometimes dinner, too.

I find myself wanting to be alone, until I am
alone, and then I find myself wanting to be with
people. It's a conundrum. When you were here,
I hardly ever saw you. But while you were way
over there in Bay St. Louis, I knew I could get
to you, or you could get to me within a little
more than hour. Much less if you were driving.
Every two weeks, you would come pick me up,
and we would go to Bob's. I think it is highly
ironic that we both continued to see him long
after our marriage ended. I think it is hilarious
that we would schedule appointments on the
same afternoon, you at 2 and me at 3. When

we'd get there, I always said, "You first," even though we both knew already that you would always go first. We tried it first the other way, and I hated it. Bob would not divulge your deepest secrets, but I picked his brain, anyway.

Bob really liked you. I think you knew that. He said you struggled with the truth, but that wasn't something I didn't know already. It seems a little sad to me that he realized our marriage was not salvageable at that point. He never said, "Get a divorce," but he encouraged me to protect my heart and not to tacitly give you permission to continue what you were doing by staying with you. That was the hardest decision I've ever had to make in my life. We started our journey with Bob in August 2013. I threw in the towel at the very end of November 2015, but it still took me months to pack my bags and leave.

I so wanted you to change your mind and what you were doing and ask me to stay. And you did. But you promised nothing about changing your behavior or activities. I got up one morning and went to brush my teeth. I didn't recognize the woman I saw in the mirror. My face was sad and drawn. I was pale and aging far more rapidly than I should have at 60. I knew that you were miserable in your own way, but you just couldn't stop. I came to understand that after three years of trying to survive in our married life that it wasn't changing for the better; it was getting worse.

I think one of the biggest differences between you and me is how we handle big issues. I had been grieving our marriage for a couple of years before we separated. You didn't begin to grieve until after I was gone. As sad as that parting was, I was ready for it. You were not.

As it turns out, though, our work on our relationship didn't really begin until after we had been separated almost a year. And it took about three more years for all the dust to settle and all the feelings to come out—out of you and out of me. I believe that there are always two sides to any marriage, just like there are in stories, and I accept my culpability in making it hard for you to be the leader. You told me a couple of times that you had regrets, but you made just as many excuses for them until the February before you died. Your valentine gift of words of truth and grace are priceless to me, and I will never, ever forget them. I only felt legitimately divorced from you the first six months or so that it became true. We talked, texted, and saw each other so much after that reality washed over us that it might as well not have been true at all.

One would think that my life was just one long parade of "what if" thoughts, but it's not. With a minor exception here and there, I have great peace. Both for you and for myself as well. I believe with my whole heart that you are with the Lord. Had you not laid it out for me that day in your apartment, when I found all your church clothes neatly arranged and ready to be worn to do the work of God, I might not have felt so certain. So, as difficult as that day was, I am grateful for it. It helped me to be easy in my heart and mind as to where you ended up in the great beyond.

I still think you're probably cheating on your golf score card.

Dear John,
A story instead of a letter:

Night of the Flaming Tacos

W e had been married less than 24 hours. You'd already gone back to Eckerd's to put in those ridiculously long hours, coming home with callouses on your right knee from kneeling on it all the time arranging endcaps.

Having just given up a job out of state, I was as yet unemployed and eager to be a proper wife.

So, I planned our first dinner.

We were dead broke. Prospects were limited. Tacos were cheap.

At the time, we hadn't moved to Dexter and were living in your funky little apartment on Laurel. Itty bitty kitchen with an apartment-sized gas stove and oven. It was my first ever gas stove and oven. I had always heard about the immediacy of its heat or the cessation thereof. Even so, I set about my task fearlessly. I am woman. Hear me bake.

It went well. For a minute.

I placed the tacos on a tray. Browned the burger and seasoned it from that little envelope full of red stuff. Shredded lettuce. Cut up tomatoes. Dumped shredded cheese into a bowl. Put out a cup of sour cream. Debated whether to put one of our only two spoons in the cup. Didn't.

I popped the taco shells into the oven just as I heard you drive up. I'd made sure I had on an apron. I felt it was important to look the part. I bounced out onto the porch and greeted you with a big smile on my face. "I made dinner," I said.

"Is that what I smell?" you asked.

It was then that I noticed tendrils of smoke curling around the door frame of the ittier bittier living room. "The taco shells!" I gasped.

I leapt across the three linear feet into the kitchen. Black, bilious smoke furled up to the ceiling and small flames slipped from the confines of the oven, licking the porcelain door, which I unfortunately flung wide open to the air. A bonfire fit for a Friday night football game pep rally ensued.

"The tacos are on fire! The tacos are on fire!" I screamed. And that was true of the ones still recognizable as taco shells. Not so much the smoldering, black husks at the back of the oven, patiently waiting to disintegrate to ash—incinerated, sacrificial food to the smirking marriage gods who were already laying down bets as to what might happen with my next meal.

You flew through the kitchen door, reached bare-handed into the oven, grabbed the baking pan, raced into the front yard, and tossed the flaming shells onto the green grass. They flickered out one by one in varying stages of scorched carbon until the last taco shell was snuffed out and darkness dropped over the lawn—a murky black blanket mercifully hiding my first culinary shame.

You did not fare so well. I turned toward you to see that your arms emanated wisps of pale smoke more alarming than our dinner. I'm pretty sure you didn't have a single hair unsinged beneath either elbow. Your fingertips were blistered and there were two bright red brands beneath each wrist.

When I saw them, I inappropriately burst forth in song, "Branded, scorned as the one who ran. What do you do when you're branded, and you know you're a man?"

You shot me a glare worthy of Chuck Connors.

My crispy hero.

We went inside, smeared triple ointment on the offended areas and invented lettuce wrapped tacos. You ate every one and declared them delicious. Exhausted from our first adventure in dinner, we tossed our paper plates (a wedding gift) into the trash can and crossed the 3 linear feet to our bed. We slept deeply and dreamt of rare filet mignon.

You had to get up at 5 a.m. to get ready for work. To make up for the night before, I crawled out of bed and made my way to the itty-bitty kitchen and burned you some eggs and toast. You left Laurel Street patting your belly and smiling—reassuring me of your willingness to support the antacid industry for as long as it took.

I followed you to the front porch, which was almost as large as our entire apartment, to see you off. There was still a hint of early morning mist, and I sniffed it to make sure it didn't smell like fricasseed taco shells.

The sun pushed through and the mist—a ghostly witness to only four hours' sleep—trailed after your beat-up red Volvo. I looked to my right. There on the lawn lay the offending shells. Each one surrounded by a tiny patch of scorched earth, the yellow grass accusing me.

I should put those in the trash, I thought.

But I yawned, turned back into the apartment, and went back to bed. On waking later, I emptied my purse of every penny, then went quarter diving into your pockets and the oldest, saddest couch in the whole world.

We ate Chinese that night.

I wore my apron. Like I'd cooked in it.

The gas stove and oven stood forlornly unused in the kitchen, as I stared at it balefully and thought, "Get used to it." You ate the last sweet and sour shrimp because I told you it was okay by me. Went to bed mad. I wanted that shrimp.

But your arms were toasted, and your fingers were covered in angry red blisters.

I sucked it up and gnawed on a dripping, red bell pepper.

The End

Letter Number Four

Dear John,

Yesterday was a month, according to the calendar, but I don't really count time that way. I count it in Sundays. You died on a Sunday morning sometime before worship started at GPC. I wasn't there. I'm sorry. Our coroner friend, Jim Faulk, described how he found you in either exquisite or excruciating detail; I change my mind about the adjective hour to hour. I made Daddy come with me to Bay St. Louis that Monday morning. We drove straight to the funeral home. I wanted to see you. I guess that's the way it is for most folks.

Lunch the Thursday before was pleasant. The food was good. As it always turned out, I wanted what you had. I can't remember what that was now. I can remember not being afraid to see you on Monday. So unadorned in death, covered by some tacky bedspread that came from who knows where. Perhaps the funeral home wasn't expecting someone to ask to see you. I made a mental note that it must have come from somewhere at Fahey, because I would never buy that kind of tacky hotel crap, and I KNOW you didn't.

I expected you to be flat on your back, but you weren't. Is it a rule that they can't change your position until the coroner decides — whatever it is that coroners decide? If Dad hadn't been standing just off my right shoulder, I would have flung myself across your body and wailed. I can't begin to explain why I didn't. Good soldier, I guess.

When there are more than thirty seconds strung together in a row, I feel seized by such profound sadness. It invades and fills my chest, pushing against my lungs like some sort of leaden balloon. I've been using the word lead a lot as of late. The sky is leaden. Food tastes bitter like lead. Everything is as cold as lead. Quilts bring me no warmth at night. I feel joined to you in death. Who knew? I've spent three and a half years thinking I was ready to go. I had cancer; you had, well, not much to complain about at the time. It never dawned on me that you might beat me to it. I battle this hoarse whisper that wheezes out of my heart at night, *Come back. Come back. Come back.* My Rose to your Jack ...

You're in a box on my desk. Such a sliver of wood for such a big, old man. I hope you're dancing over a hundred eagles and at least one hole in one by now. You realize, of course, that no one down here would believe you. Oh, you guys told such a pack of lies on the golf course. I bet God says you can't cheat on your score card, anymore. I bet you do it, anyway. I'd give a million bucks for the one Joey kept where he finally gave up counting swings and started recording cuss-word occurrences instead. I know he'll read this post. Bet he smiles, too.

Letter Number Five

Dear John,

Your birthday was Tuesday. You would have been 72. I knew it would be a tough day for all of us, so throughout the day, we posted things about you that made us laugh or that we admired about you. That done, I began to wonder what it is about the living that seem bent on sainting the dead, as if all your faults and flaws, sins of omission and commission, melt away like rendered fat in the heat. And suddenly, you are a wonder to behold as a human being. Well, I am officially UN-nominating you for sainthood. You weren't one, you know. I know.

This won't be a letter of complaint lodged against you in the celestial court, where you must prove me wrong. Just because you are residing with the Lord, I don't think He should give you an undue advantage now. Forgive me, Lord, for pointing out that the statistical odds that this ratio might change now, no matter

the new senior golfing community in which
You have placed John, seem slim to me.

I meant everything I said on your birthday,
especially the part where I gave you credit
that Stitch continued to live after that night
when we came home from church, and he had
unstuffed our brand-new Pottery Barn couch.
In truth, that exercise in lauding your merits
made a huge difference in how I handled your
birthday. Your children had saved voicemails
from you and listened to them throughout
the day, so that even though we talked about
meatball subs with lots of olives on your end
and your crying over A League of Their Own
(I thought there was no crying—especially in
baseball), their day was more forlorn than mine.

It did me good, I think, to remember other
things about you, too. Things that don't make
me miss you one whit less, but that bleed out
some of the sap, freeing up my emotional tree
trunk from becoming crystallized in grief on
the inside. I wonder if I will ever again go a
day without thinking, "Wait til I tell John this
one." My text life now genuinely sucks. My
novel lies unread and verbose in its Pages
file with no one to help me cull it and offer
meaningful insight. But I am still writing.

It dawned on me recently how heartbreaking
it would be if you have now forgotten us. We

want your joy to be complete and have chosen
to believe that you do remember us but only
the best parts—how smart the kids are, what
loving parents they have turned out to be,
how proud you are that I can now wield a
hammer and change out a toilet seat—those
things that bring joy when you love someone.
Surely a God who loves and redeems His
children would give us that small hope as
a part of the more significant hope of our
reconciliation to and resurrection with Him.

I will ache less if I know our text life
has just moved to a level that requires faith
and patience on my end and the certainty
of hearing your knowing laughter over your
maudlin, mushy family and friends when I
see you next. There must be honor in grief.
Ours because we care enough to endure such
a difficult and shifting rite of passage. And
yours because you have finished the race,
bum ticker and all. Not so bum now, though.
I really do like that part, knowing you are no
longer constantly fatigued and often in pain.

Did you meet anybody interesting today?
Shoot par? Joey has your clubs. Jordan just
bought some and starts lessons soon.

That place in our hearts where our memories
of you live is still raw. But I both see and feel
snippets of movement in the direction where

that ache is making room for the warmth which
will eventually become the sentry to that door
I enter when you come to mind. I embrace
that eventuality in my heart. It's helpful.

Letter Number Six

Dear John,

Here's the thing, hon. The next person that cocks their head at me and remarks, "I thought y'all were divorced!" is in for a good smacking. I'm trying to practice Zen grief. I really am. In more lucid moments here and there, I remember that it must be confusing for others to stand at the far end of our relationship and try to figure out why I just keep on talking about you and talking to you. On Facebook, for heaven's sake!

"Where is your dignity?"

"Your sense of privacy?"

"I thought y'all were divorced!"

You have the great luxury of having passed. You don't have to grapple with the complications that remain after 36+ years, explaining/not explaining how the knots have slowly untangled of late and then—poof! You get to be over it. I get to envision collective eye rolls and a lecture or two upon tapping "Post."

I'm trying to remember when I stopped crying. Maybe 2013. It seems like centuries now, but the day of your memorial was like a little oasis in a long stretch of tearlessness. I cried only as much as I did then because I was so moved and surprised at who and how many showed up. A past friend said I blessed her once with tears in an emotional desert of her own. Your friends were my blessing that day.

I caught my big toe on the lip of the car door two nights ago and popped my nail right off the top of my foot. Didn't cry. Worked on my vocabulary but didn't cry. Was unpacking some stuff the other day and dropped and broke a piece I really liked. Didn't cry. Found a mouse behind the couch that Frank had done in. Scooped it into a bag. Its tail fell off. Gagged but didn't cry (you know how much I like a house mouse). A couple of projects that I put a lot of effort into flopped. Haven't cried. It is a curiosity to me. Think back to the way I'd react once upon a time when somebody won money on Wheel of Fortune. I'm for sure not crying over baseball, anymore. That's your gig. Strange days, indeed.

I'm officially your widow now. Even though we were divorced. The government says so, therefore, it must be true.

I dare anybody to say different. A good smacking might be in order..

Dear John,
    A story instead of a letter:

Early

Childbirth. My first. I was utterly unprepared, as I am sure most first-time mothers find themselves to be. We had no idea about the sex of our child. Neither of us wanted to spoil the surprise of having our obstetrician hoist our baby into the air and declare, "It's a boy!" Not to brag, but I already knew that I was carrying a man-child. I had a hunch, and my hunches are usually spot on.

Like many parents of that decade, we had been to several Lamaze classes. We had practiced relaxation techniques and breathing and watched a film about childbirth that almost made both of us pass out. I think I did throw up in my mouth a little. For the first time, I asked quite seriously, "Um, can I take a bye on this part?" Baleful glare. Our Lamaze instructor didn't suffer fools lightly. I was supposed to be rejoicing over the process that would put a small human in our arms, so that we could buy cute little outfits with bears and bunnies on them. Not be a big crybaby.

I was due October 5, 1983. On the night of August 13, 1983, I awoke, thinking my bladder was pretty full, and that I needed to get out of bed and go take care of business. By the time I got to the hallway, my water broke. Ew. I waddled back to bed and shook your shoulder. You looked at me blearily, and I whispered like we were in the library, "I think the baby's coming."

Your kids, Matt and Nicole, were with us that weekend, so the most immediate concern was what to do about that. We couldn't take them with us. We couldn't leave them alone. So, we called the worst baby sitter we knew, your mom, to come and stay with the kids while we trundled off to the hospital to bring a little man-child into the world. (I was right by the way; I said my hunches are usually spot on.) When your mom got to the house, I had packed my little suitcase with virtually nothing that would prove helpful over the next few days, except for my toothbrush and a clean pair of underwear. No toothpaste, socks, or clothes in which to come home.

We had that little Triumph, remember? Cramming my swollen, pregnant body into a sports car meant for willowy, sleek European women was quite the challenge. But you loved that car and had a special hat you referred to as your "go to hell" hat that you wore every time you got behind the wheel. I'd seen you drive fast before, but that night, I ruined the upholstery on the passenger side by clenching the armrest so hard, the leather covering cracked.

About the time we were careening around the curve at Dauphin and Monterey on just two wheels, it dawned on me that it was a mite early to be barreling toward Providence Hospital at the speed of light. Wasn't I due a month and a half later than this? I was not about to distract you by pointing this out. Your jaw was set, and what difference would it make? You'd have looked in my direction to be sure I wasn't kidding, we'd have crashed into a telephone pole and died on the eve of the most joyous occasion of our lives, the birth of our firstborn.

I'm pretty sure Dexter Avenue was about 15 minutes from Providence Hospital on Springhill on a day without traffic. We made the drive in six minutes flat. When my attention was not wildly distracted with contractions, I was sufficiently diverted by the need to hang on hard enough not to be ejected from the car. You had the top down.

A lot of what happened between that moment and being in the pre-delivery room having real, live, not-a-happy-moment contractions is kind of blurry. But I have exquisitely clear memories of what happened from that point on. We had chosen our OB/GYN on the basis of his being one of your cronies from college. A scant recommendation. I didn't quite think that one through. "Chip" was in a solo practice, I wasn't due, and he was out of town, so the delivery doctor from Hades entered the room. I got a thorough chewing out because my records were not to be found at the hospital. When I claimed I wasn't due for another six weeks, he chewed me out basically by insinuating that I was either an idiot or a liar.

You know how hot natured I am. But I hadn't brought the socks I had been instructed to bring in the few Lamaze classes we had made it through, and my feet were cold. When I asked you to call my ex-husband to bring me my big, wooly red socks that I hadn't claimed when we divorced, the look of incredulity on your face was classic. Wish I could have taken a picture, but there were more immediate concerns. It was a very short labor. At 6 centimeters, everyone—nurses, doctor, and you—left the room to suit up, and there I lay in an attractive hospital gown in no underwear and without my big, wooly, red socks, which you had resolutely refused to call and get for me. The delivery nurse assured me I had plenty of time to writhe around in searing and ferocious agony while you guys put on flimsy little suits designed to do I have no idea what.

Here's the thing for which I almost can't forgive you. After everyone was gone, and I was practicing my Lamaze breathing technique for transitional labor, I couldn't remember where my focal point was, and transitional labor descended upon me with a vengeance. I think I was supposed to take a long breath through my nose and then exhale in two short breaths followed by a longer breath to ease the pain and give me something else to focus on rather than the focal point I could not find. The leviathan in my belly had better come out shortly, or I would surely die.

About the time you came back into the room, I only remember that I had signed on for an epidural, not natural childbirth, and I wanted that epidural. For the rest of our lives together, you lied like a dog about how I asked for it. When you returned, you said I'd have failed the breathing class. I sounded like a freight train, according to you. Rather than hee hee hoo, I was raised up as high as I could get over my gargantuan belly shouting, "Whoo! Whoo! Whoo!" like a freight train roaring into the station. You said.

I spoke calmly to you. I'm sure my voice was intense, but I maintain that my head did not spin completely around on my shoulders. I did not grab you by the collar of your shirt and jerk your face down to mine. And I certainly did not sound like Mercedes Cambridge when I yelled, "I WANT MY EPIDURAL!!!"

Too late, the nurse informed me. Our baby was coming and coming that very moment. Somehow, I managed to wriggle my way off the pre-delivery room bed and onto a gurney that was wheeled into the delivery room right about the time our son's head crowned. "Am I going to have a baby in the hallway?" I wondered. What if he popped out when I was halfway between the gurney and the delivery table? WHERE WAS MY DADBURNED EPIDURAL? The doctor flew into the delivery room like Paul Harvey, ready to broadcast the birth at a moment's notice. When he realized that a baby was about to be born when he didn't even have his gloves on, he got very snippy with the nurses. I didn't care. I just wanted whatever was churning inside me to get out, out, out.

I absolutely do believe you when you tell me that I looked at you with the most intense and violent loathing and whistled between my clenched teeth, "I hate you. Don't you ever touch me again."

The reason many women have second and third children is because we are told we forget the pain of childbirth and remember only the joy of holding that little darling in our arms for the first time. Eww. Thank God Joey was born before folks started videoing every, tiny, distasteful detail. Although that might have attested to my veracity about the whole *Exorcism* scene.

After Joey escaped my tired body, they cleaned him up a little, declared that he had an under-average Apgar (Really? At six weeks early?), they passed him cautiously over to you, so that you could show me what we had produced in a mere seven-and-a-half months. After all, had you not vibrated the umbilical cord in two with a pair of scissors handed to you by Dr. Nasty? Of course, you should have the privilege of showing me our baby boy.

You stuck his baby butt in my face. I wasn't at all sure what kind of reaction that should elicit, because by that time, I wasn't at all sure which end you were showing me. He was whisked away by the nurses and carried to the nursery, so he could be examined to make sure his little lungs were functioning properly. At that point, I hadn't heard anybody say he had all ten fingers and ten toes. But the boy had a butt.

I was absolutely sure about that.

Letter Number Seven

Dear John,

Right now, I am hot and sweaty and sorely aggravated, and I don't even know what number this letter is. I'm on a train to Toulouse, which isn't even where I'm supposed to be going. Not happy about that AT ALL!!

Phew! That's off my chest.

I had an epiphany/realization/divine revelation this past Saturday. I thought I'd let you know that France is not what I thought it would be. And I blame you. Yes, you. And don't give me that *"What did I do?"* look (I mean it—don't). I have dreamed and dreamed about this trip for so long, I don't even remember how old I was when I started working on my French accent. I remember lying flopped on my stomach crossways on the bed, giving it my best shot (out loud, of course). Mom was walking down the hallway past my bedroom and burst out laughing. Embarrassing, yes, but I kept at it. Despite winding up taking four years of German, my intention to inhabit

France, no matter how briefly, never wavered.
I began studying the language in earnest
in March. Guess what? I suck at French.

Here's the thing:

I still have moments every day when
small eddies of sadness wash across my
heart. Don't be offended, but I haven't
been wallowing in grief since you died.
Even so, I can't quite avoid little spasms of
awareness each day that you are ... absent.

When you died, a 38-year streak of
conversations died with you. Countless inside
jokes. Faces that no one else can read. Pillow
talk, even though you NEVER left it on the
pillow, blabbermouth. My likes, my dislikes,
my fears, my pleasures, our shared memories
... Seriously ... my history died with you.
There is no one here to appreciate the depth
of expertise I have achieved in sporting
a perfect French accent without actually
being able to speak recognizable French.

I can't call you. I can't text you. I can't save
up funny stories and peeves to tell you about
later. I've heard married people say a zillion
times that their spouses were their best friends.
Well, we were friends and then we weren't and
then we were again. And even though I can
relate many things to some other person, no one
will hear it or respond to it the way you would
have with our whole history of experiences

together behind the telling of the tale. It would take me eons to explain to anyone else why it was so weird or funny or memorable. And it would still fall flat without those myriad layers of paint slathered onto our mutual canvas.

I suppose that's the problem for surviving partners of long-standing relationships. The vacuum left by your absence didn't cease after your memorial. All the current events of my life now sort of sift skyward like wisps of smoke because the ears and heart that would hear them most clearly and significantly are gone. To whom do I relate these minutiae or epic moments now?

So. Here I sit. On a train to Toulouse. In France. The French countryside is rolling past at who knows how many kilometers per hour as dusk is confused with the tunnels that shut out the scenery and the light. When I get to Toulouse, which is not where I'm supposed to be going, I will make my way to a hotel and collapse into bed. I'm absolutely positive I will pick up my phone to text you a very long grouse. If you were *here*, you wouldn't be here, so a text would have to do me.

I've never minded striking out into the unknown by myself. I'd have been in France sans spouse even if you were still alive and I'd begged you to come. Your armchair might have had an anxiety attack and required hospitalization. I'd still like to grouse-text you. Send you pretty pictures and tell you how mal I find French food so far. Tease you about sneaking over to Austria when no one is looking. There's a girl across the aisle with a spiral notebook writing vast quantities of verbiage in blue, back-slanted ink. She has pretty brown skin and has her hair pulled up into what I swear is a French twist. How apropos. (Does that count as French?) We'd be talking about her late tonight. I'd be reading tone of voice into your text. You'd be telling me to go to sleep. Henri would be going berserk when you spoke my name out loud.

As it is, I'll just go to bed. All my travels and adventures validated only against the drop cloth that bears images of my mental checklist. France. Check. French. Not check. But tres amusante, non?

Letter Number Eight

Dear John,

It occurs to me that every time I have moved in the last four years, it follows on the heels of some kind of intense stress or tragedy. There have been marriage woes, cancer, and death sandwiched between 2016 and 2019. As I've emptied each house of whatever it is I've collected since I got there, I have left some sorrowful and painful memories in the empty spaces. And I won't miss a one of them. Except maybe you.

I've learned one lesson for sure in life—never say never. I moved again this week. Further out in the country where there are horses and mules and chickens and beehives and lots of wild geese that fly so close to the back porch that you can hear the wind whooshing out from beneath their wings. It is a small house, but it's mine. I know you would like it, but it's not exactly what we talked about. It's been cold and dreary and miserable the last several days, but on the first warm and sunny day, I will sit out on the back

porch and drink my first cup of coffee here,
in honor of the history of all the moves that
have come about before, during, and after you.

I dare to hope, despite all evidence to the
contrary, that this is my last move. I hope
this is my final home on Planet Earth. I hope
never to see another dust bunny the size of
Arizona hiding behind the bed, along with
several earrings I forgot to take off before I
went to sleep and lost just that one. I hope
never to have to pack another box and cram it
into the back of my car. I hope never to have
to unpack that same box and have newspaper
ink all over my hands, only half of which will
come off with one washing in warm, soapy
water. I hope never to have to figure out how
to arrange heavy furniture that absolutely no
one wants to come and help me move around
the same room several times. I hope never
to have to wonder why it didn't occur to me
to mark "Kitchen—Pots and Pans" on boxes
rather than just "Kitchen," as this is completely
ineffectual when you are looking for your pots
and pans, and they are seven insurmountable
rows deep in the back of the garage, and
they're all marked "Kitchen." I hope never to
have to watch Nala wander around the house
trying to figure out where she is NOW and to
constantly guard the door in order to keep her
in the house and out of the danger of getting

lost in a world full of big horse's hooves and suspiciously nefarious roosters. And I REALLY hope never to have to take down, move, and rehang "Peasant Wedding" ever again.

But these are just hopes I have.

I honestly don't know why anyone would voluntarily submit to the home-buying process if they knew in advance what all that entails. It was the realization of most every kind of nightmare I could entertain in a dream. I like to have my ducks in a row, but mortgage brokers don't use ducks; they use cats. And herding them is every bit as much fun as you can imagine it might be. But there was a moment, brief but memorable, when I signed a bottom line that went onto a deed that will be recorded in Chancery Court that says this house belongs to Marcia Byars Willett. And that would be me.

However, it would be way more satisfying to listen to you grouse and moan for days about having to move "Peasant Wedding" for the eleventy-somethingth time.

Love,

Letter Number Nine

Dear John,

My crosses were in an awful tangle. I've snatched one off the hook in haste on so many Sunday mornings, the ones left hanging got into a fearful knot. So, I did impatiently what you used to do so painstakingly. One and a half hours picking chains and leather apart, making progress, making new knots, making my old eyes ache and sting. I think my eyes are the oldest part of me. I'm amazed at what I can't see without my glasses these days. There's not a Bible on Amazon that has print big enough to overcome that little handicap. It makes me sadder than my hands do.

You know my bad habit of falling asleep with the television on. 4:33 a.m. is now my witching hour. I woke up to Episode 1 of "The Pillars of the Earth" yesterday before dawn yawned itself to light. I am now binging. You remember how assiduously I've avoided reading that series. Now I'm going to have to. Most of your books are still boxed up in the carport. I wonder if they are in the boxes or if they were on your iPad? I'll look tomorrow.

I didn't write on Father's Day. It was too hard. More because I knew how much more painful the day was for Joey and Jordan than for me. Not that it was easy. Just harder for them, I know.

I wonder how long it will be before I stop checking shirt sizes when I see one I know would look good on you? I know you're all decked out in blinding white, but there are still some pretty pink shirts out there. I've perfected the selfie eye roll on that proclivity. Kohl's thinks I am hilarious.

Every single day I want to talk to you. Of course, I do but you don't answer back. I want to sit across the table and pick at your lunch because it always looks tastier than mine. I want to argue theology. I want to grouse to someone who won't hold it against me. Or remind me of it when I get past it.

You must be marveling at your strong gait and beating heart. That will be a sight to behold one day. I'll be able to see you 20/20!

Dear John,
 A story instead of a letter:

The Way Home

Steve Ramp kept us in hot water. Months before we had finished our training for the lay pastor's program, he thought it might be a good idea for us to go talk to the people at Westminster in Natchez. Their interim needed to step down, the church was small and struggling. Ramp thought maybe we could energize an elderly congregation between the two of us 'cuz we were so sparkly. I'm pretty sure that just means they were too broke to hire a "real" minister. Maybe Westminster would be willing to entertain the idea of a completely untried husband and wife team looking for some church willing to entertain crazy for a while. We drove up during the week to talk with their session. You and all the guys got along like gangbusters. But the all-male church leaders were quite vocal about their feelings toward having a woman in a leadership position— even one shared with a big, furry bald man a foot and a half taller than anybody else in any room. I could tell they wanted you.

You were so much more charismatic than me. I had my own sparkle, but it lurked somewhere a little deeper under the surface. I could talk to anyone, but I warmed up slowly. You could talk to a fence post and come away satisfied that you had made a "close, personal friend."

Westminster wound you up. You were a race-horse at the gate, straining against the six months of classes yet to be completed, heart pounding with desire to get in the race. You were coming up from the rear and there was a lot of catching up to do.

Westminster was interested but wanted to hear us preach. Okay. You first. You second, honestly. Third, fourth, and fifth would have been fine with me, but they asked you to preach after Christmas, and I got—Transfiguration Sunday. Oh, joy. Not just some regular sermon, but one centered on the glorification of Christ as He had a pow wow with Moses and Elijah in the presence of his best buds. Wow. Piece of cake. No problem. You were completely unsympathetic to my plight. I don't think you ever realized how terrifying the prospect of preaching the gospel in any circumstance was to me. It was one thing to teach kids improper placement of a comma, but we were talking about keeping the congregation informed as to the activities and purposes of the Son of God! Heaven or hell was in the balance. I was not prepared to be responsible for parlaying the effective salvation of anyone's soul. I wasn't even sure about the tenure of my own faith.

I virtually made Steve Ramp write that sermon. He laid out the framework, and I tried to rewrite it in my own words, using our mutual experiences from a spiritual renewal weekend we had all attended. Even trying to read it out loud in your presence made me queasy. I KNEW how hard it was going to be serving as a female cleric in Mississippi. My closest friend was the first female Presbyterian minister installed in the State of Mississippi in our denomination. At that time, I think there were three female solo pastors in the entire state. Even with you as co-pastor, I didn't think I stood a chance.

And I didn't want to.

I had been fighting against the concept of becoming a pastor from Day One. That was your dream. All the way back to your post-Vietnam War days, you had dreamed of being a minister. You had started seminary in Tennessee. But Wife Number One wasn't having it, so you left seminary and went to work selling toilet paper. Big, big accounts in big, big toilet paper business, but it was still toilet paper. I can't speak to the death of that marriage. I wasn't there. But I was there not too many years after you divorced. My experience with Wife Number One was significantly less than pleasant. She made the skin of my teeth feel funny. It got so bad at one point, that I got an almanac and marked in red the day thirteen years in the future on which our last child support/alimony payment was due. Year by year, we worked on loving and keeping your kids in our lives, but kids become teenagers, and teenagers think parents are incredibly uncool. Especially parents who live in another state. But I greatly admired that you were willing to give up your life's dream for your family, even though your family fell apart shortly thereafter.

Then suddenly when you were 59 years old, God poured ministry in your lap like molten gold by offering you the opportunity to become a lay pastor. We had to go to lay pastor's school. For a year and a half, one weekend a month, in six different aspects of ministerial work. You were having the time of your life. I felt like a tadpole in a pool full of sharks. It wasn't my thing. I knew in my heart it wasn't my thing. I tried over and over to tell you and Ramp that it wasn't my thing. That I had no intention of going into ministry. I was a teacher, not a preacher.

Neither of you ever heard a word I said.

I think it was John Dudley who told us that Sundays roll around with relentless regularity. He wasn't lying. Transfiguration Sunday barreled through time, turning days into hours and hours into moments. And the moment arrived. We drove to Natchez, shook a lot of hands of people I will never remember. You would. Every, single one. I was so far past nervous that I thought Webster's should invent a new word for what I was feeling. I wasn't afraid. I was prophetic. It was going to be a disaster, and you know how I feel about my hunches.

I mounted the chancel and took my seat to the right of the pulpit. There was probably a music minister there. I don't remember. I don't remember where the interim was seated. I don't remember even knowing where you were seated until a mere breath into the sermon. I don't even remember if I was the liturgist or whether someone else read the scriptures. Most everything about that morning falls into the category of selective amnesia. I wish I could say that I forgot that I was even there, but all those murky uncertainties about who was what and where coalesced into one acutely focused moment. When it happened, I found your face in the space of one heartbeat.

When the music stopped (don't ask me what we were singing), I stepped to the pulpit. I grabbed either side in a death grip. I looked out over the congregation with blind eyes and launched into the first words I knew for opening a sermon, and they are the same words I use today. I'm pretty sure I cadged those from Ramp.

"Grace and peace to you from God our Father and our Lord Jesus Christ."

Had I gone and sat down that very moment, perhaps things would have fallen out differently.

But I had taken a deep breath and come to the realization that my mouth was so dry, I might not be able to speak another word. I begged God to drop a Hall's onto the pulpit, already unwrapped, so I could just surreptitiously pop it into my mouth and have enough spit to utter the next sentence. As this thought scrolled across my brain, an older couple about halfway to the back of the church in the middle section of pews stood up quietly. They didn't look at me. I think they kept their eyes down altogether. Without speaking, they slipped quietly out of the pew and left the sanctuary.

Had I unknowingly uttered a curse word in the middle of my opening blessing? Was something hanging out of my nose? Did I sound like a Yankee? You've heard me preach; you know Yankee was not the problem.

There may or may not have been a significant pause. I don't remember that, either. I do remember finding your face on the front row on the pews to my left. I do remember trying to wither you with a mere glance, then a stare, and then an outright challenge not to look at me when I was hating you from the pulpit. You'd have thought it was child labor all over again. I didn't say anything out loud, but I'm sure you got the gist of it.

I had actually taken my cell phone up to the pulpit, because I was using it as a visual aid. I talked about the busyness of life and how little time we carved out of our day to be in the presence of the Lord. My sermon could have been 20 minutes or 2 seconds. If you weren't gone, you could help me remember that. I guess I'll never know. I don't remember one word past "cell phone."

We talked with the session members afterwards. The ladies of the church had prepared a light lunch for us, so we were able to chat with members of the congregation, who were all unfailingly kind in their assessment of my sermon. Someone had made cake! I was given a piece. I think I snorted it. I mournfully watched the cake be whittled down to nothing. My plans to swipe it, go hide in the bathroom, and consume it in short order were whisked away like the last piece, given to a lovely lady with silver hair twisted up in the back in a knot. I was not exuding the milk of Christian kindness at the moment. My best thought was she had probably slept through the whole sermon. Therefore, she did not deserve the remaining crumbs of the cake. I needed to induce a sugar coma and escape the realities of all that I already knew and had long predicted about my future as a pastor.

The check they gave me I quietly deposited into an offering plate at the back of the sanctuary before we left. It nestled there among all the other folded checks, dollar bills, twenties, and a single one-hundred-dollar tucked discreetly beneath all the other offerings.

It seemed only fair that Natchez was the only place you were going to reach if you were going to

Natchez. You could cross the bridge into Vidalia, Louisiana, and grab a few onions, but other than that, you had to be prepared to put in some time on the road to reach any other destination. Natchez was a place solely unto itself.

And it was a long ride home to Pascagoula, Mississippi. You could not have enjoyed the drive. I certainly didn't. We tortured each other mile marker by mile marker. We sounded like 5-year-olds discussing whether I actually belonged in ministry.

"Do not."

"Do, too."

"Do not."

"Do, too."

There were more words. A plethora of words changed places, hissed out in the confines of your truck, because my car wasn't fit to make the trip. I could usually argue you into silence with ease, but you weren't having it that Sunday afternoon. I finally lost my cool— a very bad idea.

"If God wants me to go into ministry," I shouted at the windshield, "He's going to have to tell me Himself!"

I meant to yell at you, but the instant the words popped out of my mouth, I knew I had just hollered at the Almighty. There were several eternal seconds of silence between us. I saw you try imperceptibly to inch toward the driver's door in case some unpleasant supernatural activity was aimed at my side. You switched on the radio and fiddled around until you found a station broadcasting some basketball game. Maybe baseball. I was confused and waiting for the whole supernatural thing to be over with, so I could be put out of my misery.

The remainder of the ride from Houma to Pascagoula played out on a lighter note.

"Where do you want to stop and grab a bite?"

"Is that Dillard's open?"

"No."

"Rats."

"Keep a lookout for a decent price on gas."

"Don't miss our turn onto I-10."

"Are you sure that Dillard's wasn't open?"

"Yep."

It was the middle of February 2009. My first and last sermon had gone down in infamy. This fact did not bother me one whit, because I thought that meant the game, while not over for John, had resulted in my being benched once and for all. Thank goodness. The session at Westminster took a pass. Thank You, God. Thank You so much. And I'm sorry I hollered at You. For a second there, I thought You were John.

A scant two days later, Ramp found another bus to throw us under. We started getting calls from churches around the Presbytery to come and preach while so-and-so was out of town or on sabbatical. You gleefully set out almost every

Sunday for months. Sometimes, I would go with you, but mostly I went to First Prez and communed with my real people. I began to hope that some church's line of sight would narrow in on you and I could just tag along and be a pastor's wife? OHN! (Don't bother trying to look that one up; I just invented it). Nope. Absolutely not. I knew a bunch of pastor's wives and 98.5% of them hated the job. A pastor's wife was a glorified gopher, and heaven forbid if she could play piano or sing. That way a church got a two-fer. One salary, two employees, one of which you didn't have to be nice to at all.

It boiled down to this. Preach or turn you loose and go solo forever at my home church. You were set to retire in a little more than a year. If you were called, it would mean lots of expensive travel or move to another location. The odds were stacked against me, and I knew it. Our next course was homiletics. God works in mysterious ways. Maybe actually preaching in front of the person trying to cram this square secular peg into some round homiletical hole would do the trick.

One could only hope.

Letter Number Ten

Dear John,

Today, I cleaned out the cat litter box. More than that, I took the whole box outside and gave it a good scrubbing. Ugh. But the litter box is impeccably clean and smells—? well, not like cat litter. I am doing so many things I never even considered as something that might be my task several years ago. If it was the least bit distasteful or icky, I'd just call your name. I might have to remind you that the garbage had to go out that night for pick up the next morning. Or that the dog (yuck) had left a deposit surely for you and not me in the hallway. You were reluctant sometimes, but you always sucked it up, scooped up poop, climbed on ladders to clean out gutters, scrubbed the toilet on days when just the thought of it made me throw up a little. I was a housework diva. You were as lazy as me but more motivated to keep the peace in the house when I was mostly interested in avoiding anything that smelled even remotely unpleasant.

Even when I was terrible at some job I had undertaken, you never condescended to me or raised Cain when, on occasion, you had every right to do that. I prided myself that in all our years of marriage, I had only called you a bad name once, and it was in a moment of great distress (no, not when I was in labor; all bets are off during labor). I never called you an idiot, a jerk, or any number of epithets that admittedly sprang to mind. In dealing with your loss, it occurs to me that you didn't call me names, either. Not once that I can remember. Even when I was very busy being exactly whatever epithet probably popped into your head. Not once.

I think this is a mark of respect in our relationship that was highly under-represented in the negotiations for the dissolution of our marriage. I thought you had little respect for me. I knew you thought I had zero respect for you. I thought I carried the burden of the most serious of responsibilities couples are supposed to share. You thought I treated you like a servant. Personally, I would have called you more of a cabana boy. Kidding! Not kidding! You were the undisputed back-scratching champion of the known universe. I would pay a massage therapist these days to scratch my back rather than smooth out my muscular kinks.

At least we thought enough of one another not to resort to name calling just to win an argument or get in the last word. Sometimes I think if we had paid more attention to the things that did work for us and less to the things that were driving us crazy, it might have turned out differently. I would argue with you when you put yourself down. I always thought you were smart, politically astute, and faithful to any job you undertook if not to me. But that's another letter.

Anyway. I now can change light bulbs even at great heights. I can run a riding mower around my little green acre. I have fixed a couple of minor plumbing problems. I CHANGED THE TOILET SEAT!!! Which means I had to get up close and personal to all my favorite parts of the toilet. I changed the refrigerator doors so that they opened from left to right when I moved onto my farmlet. I'm still learning. Hanging drapes, for reasons I can't explain, is a lot more fun if you know how to hang the curtain rods and not have to holler for someone to come over and help. Not that I don't have to do that occasionally. I like it less and less, though, so I work extra hard to accomplish it on my own. I'm not just a part-separating sidekick, anymore. I'm in charge of construction. I am woman. Hear me drill.

I can't live a life full of "what ifs," so I try hard not to dwell on how things might have been had we only ...

During the days when your memories lean
to the sainted side, I remind myself of those
things that did separate us. I remind myself
that you went almost a decade without even
giving me a card on our anniversary or my
birthday. There seems to be a measure of
unfairness in being the one left behind to ponder
all these things. So, I guess that's a grievance
I'm airing. Not about our past but about my
present. I haven't gotten to a point, yet, where
I can put you out of my mind for a whole 24
hours. If I'm going to obsess, I'm going to give
myself some good reasons not to roll around in
the dirt, beating myself up for all my marital
shortcomings. When you died, we had been
divorced for more than two years. Both of us
had garnered a good deal of living alone under
our belts. I was just better at it than you were.

But that space between going and coming
turned out to be invaluable. Since I can't afford
to think about where we might have gone had
you not died in the middle of a bunch of plans,
I choose to pinch myself just hard enough to
jar my thoughts away from a future that will
never happen now. Because you died. Jerk.

Letter Number Eleven

Dear John,

I wasn't going to write this letter until
Friday. On Friday, you will have been gone
for ten months. I decided when the clock
struck midnight that there is a great deal
of silliness in waiting to write a letter to
you just because you haven't quite been
dead for ten whole months, so, I am writing
it tonight, or this morning. Whatever.

If I were to go back through all the previous
letters, I would most likely discover that I tend
to dash one of these off around the monthly
"anniversary" of your death. You've been gone
ten months, and this is letter #11. But just
after the first of the year, I penned a letter to
your children rather than to you. It took me
two hours and was around 2300 words long.
You know me, I can't say it in shorthand if I
am serious about it. It was a lovely, long letter.
I told them about where I find myself now and
what I value about my life and about them and
about our combined histories. I wrote about

my desire for them to be happy and fulfilled in
their own lives and the lives of their children.
I wrote about how much I admired and loved
them and told them why. I had literally just
typed, "Love, Mom," and brushed the text to
scroll to the top, and the whole darn thing just
disappeared, never to be seen again. I thought
the rules of computers were that you can't ever
get rid of anything. Apparently, the one loophole
is writing meaningful, heartfelt letters to your
children on or about New Year's to serve as some
sort of living will. Poof! Gone forever. You'd
have loved that letter. It was life-affirming.

Mostly, these days, I am okay. Then, like
a sudden gust of wind, you will brush across
my mind and stir up and scatter the leaves
of memories that are sweet, bittersweet, or
just bitter. I have occasionally forced myself
to remember some of the more despicable
moments in our history just to stem the
tide of any emotional response, because you
know I do not like that. For all that may
seem contrary to that notion, you better than
anyone else, know/knew (how do I refer to
your presence now?) that I can't stand to be
manipulated by emotions. I still have a standing
rule that no movie will ever make me cry.

Nor will you.

I've been in the new house since December
13. And ... I ... am ... still ... unpacking. Ugh!

This makes dodging your presence almost impossible. Every single box has something in it that compels me to think of a moment in time in which that item was somehow significant to both of us. I went almost an entire week without thinking of you in the hallway, and hearing my mind say, "Oh, Honey," hoping I'd found you just sleeping there.

There are times of self-reflection when I wonder if one day there is going to be a gully washer. And it will all come pouring out with a relentless ferocity that mirrors the clamor, the litany I recite when stepping to the side of any emotional traffic jam, that I use to stem my tendency toward a morbid fascination with the space between living and dying.

I got a text message yesterday that Anne Blair died just a day or so ago. And I didn't have anyone to tell that it would have mattered to at all. I sent her daughter a message that you had moved on as well. Even though she had spoken to someone at Old Town, she had no idea that you were gone.

I will miss her for the both of us.

Love,

Dear John,
    A story instead of a letter:

Dead Dog

My daddy always said, "You're old enough to where your wants won't hurt you." I suppose that's true, but when I fell in love with something, I'd grind my teeth trying to figure out a way to make it mine. Tenacity is not always a good thing.

We have already established that you are euphemistically frugal (I'll always say, "read cheap"). You notoriously preferred eating toxic cheese sandwiches (Velveeta, eww) every day for the rest of your life rather than take me out for a cheap Chinese dinner. That doesn't mean, of course, that we didn't eat a lot of Chinese food. I was persuasive, and if that didn't work, I had a world class sad puppy face. The last step beyond sad puppy face was a classic Southern hissy fit, something you assiduously avoided.

True confession. I have a serious addiction to Pottery Barn.

We had been in the ministry for about three years, I guess. We were living in a house on

Ramoneda, way too big for us, with those 30-foot ceilings that showed up on our electric bill every single month with the ferocity of a hungry money -eating beast.

Our couch had suffered the tortures of the damned between two dogs and two cats and a long history of other abuses. I declared it to be irretrievably ratty. Your response was a deep, defeated sigh. You knew right away that there would be a new couch in the house before Christmas.

We did talk about it. Remember, we talked about it. What did we want? Formal? Contemporary? Casual? Cheap? Oh, no, my dear. On sale maybe but not cheap. Even though we made typical pastor's pay, I had been saving a frequent-flyer's coupon to Pottery Barn and was daily stalking sales for hefty discounts. You at least have to give me that. I never paid retail. Of course, if it cost more than $1.95, your display of the boy version of a classic hissy fit was in the making.

Why not try a sectional, we wondered? We'd never had one before, mostly because they left me with the impression of belonging in a bachelor's apartment. A bachelor with nefarious intentions and bad taste. But the times, they were a'changin'. We had so much company, we needed to capitalize on places for people to sit. The annual session Christmas banquet was right around the corner. I had a brilliant idea.

Let's rent one and see if we like it!

You had your own arsenal of doomed expressions: eye rolling, defeated sighs, head hung low. I was far more impervious to yours than you were to mine.

So, I trundled off to the furniture rental store and looked around. Yuck. Two more stores. Double yuck. Finally, at the last place I stopped, I found a sectional that wasn't too offensive, although it was lumpy and way too fluffy. But not hideous, so I arranged for a delivery date, and you and I dragged our living room couch out into the sunroom and hid it around the corner, where the dogs immediately discovered that they could wreak havoc, and no one was going to yell at them.

The delivery day came; the ginormous sectional was squeezed through our front door and deposited into the middle of the room. I thought it was homely but had to admit the shape was a good fit with our other furniture and offered far more seating space than had our beleaguered post-Katrina clunker. We lived with it for about two weeks and decided, mutually, I might add, to seek one out to buy. I knew exactly where it would come from. When the rental had come for a visit, I began scanning Pottery Barn couches in earnest to see what was out there and how painful it would be to have it delivered to 809 Ramoneda Avenue.

Painful.

But I was undeterred and managed to fall in in love with a neutral, scaled down version of the behemoth in the living room. It was not cheap. I stalked that couch every day for a month. It went on sale but only with a 20% discount. Not yet. It went on sale about two weeks later with a 25% discount. Hmmmm. Combined with my coupon that would come to ... whoa. Not yet. Then I had another brilliant idea. I called customer service, and we talked a long time about how much money I had spent with Pottery Barn over the years and the couch would be the most expensive item I had ever purchased from them. They connected me with a design specialist. She was very sympathetic to my cause. I shamelessly pointed out the lowly situation pastors, especially co-pastors, dealt with financially and that our need to seat company was a prima fascia case for the need to have a sleek, wheat-colored, comfy Pottery Barn couch come live at our house.

She gave me another 5% off. Combined with my coupon, that meant $1500 off PB's exorbitant price. I TOLD you it was expensive. I may be a spendthrift, but I do not lie about it. You still had a minor version of a stroke. But I was actually very proud that I had negotiated the price down to way too expensive as opposed to ridiculously unaffordable and out of our reach. Sort of.

I was a lot more excited when the permanent addition to our household arrived. We had been talking to the animals for a week, threatening them with all manner of death and mayhem if they so much as looked at that couch. We settled it in the living room. It looked fabulous! I knew you thought so, too, because you declared it "okay." But you still refused to sit on it, preferring your recliner, the true love of your life, to the sexy sueded wheat fabric. So, I luxuriated on it all by myself.

We had gone through a string of crazy land-ladies since selling our home. But Ramoneda's landlady took the cake. When we received the cata-strophic $780 power bill in August of that year, we decided to take her offer of an early termination. (Her new relationship with a beau in California hadn't worked out, and she wanted to come home). We wanted a smaller house with lower ceilings.

We found a small 3/2 right down from the beach that was a whole $100 cheaper than the monstrosity we were escaping. But it had an inter-esting layout and two of the bedrooms opened out onto the back patio through double French doors.

Before we moved, I managed to fall in love with a little runt Frenchbo we named Stitch, because he looked just like the adorable, little alien in the animated film *Stitch and Lilo*. He was very, very cute. Which is good, because it enabled him to live a lot longer than he might have had his ears not been huge and his little smush face completely mischievous and irresistible. When we moved into the smaller house, you bemoaned the fact that the yard was very tiny and turning two boxers, a hybrid hot mess named Stitch, and Billcat and

Chloe loose in it was going to prove challenging, since there wasn't a lot of running around room in the house, either. You were always sooo skeptical. I told you we'd be just fine. Despite the fact that Sam and Karmen were convinced Stitch was the devil's henchman. Our vet Charlie had to put Sam on Prozac for his nerves, remember? We came home from church one afternoon, and poor Sam was practically comatose on the floor, drooling. We had to pick him up and put him—sigh—on the couch. I threw a blanket over it first and you settled him gently onto some very expensive cushions.

Thus, our doom was sealed.

From that day on, the dogs were convinced we had bought them an extremely comfortable, classy dog bed. We couldn't keep any of them off it even when we were in the room. So, sadly, you helped me drape sheets and blankets all over it to protect it from three dogs and two cats. We were so foolishly optimistic and naive.

Every Wednesday, you and I put in very long days, probably about ten hours each. There was Bible study in the morning, dinner, and another Bible study at night. Plus, all the other attendant duties of pastors punched into the moments not consumed by studies, dinners, and more studies.

The Wednesday I remember most acutely, we were running late. We'd been cornered by AJ. You laughed at me from behind his back as I worked my way all the way to the wall and tried to flatten myself into the cracks of the paneling to avoid being spit on by someone whose sense of personal space amounted to about 2 inches. You said you were pretty sure you saw my face go concave as spit sought it out. He was harmless, I know. And you were mean to laugh at me when AJ couldn't see you. A real husband would have intervened and suffered having his tie spit on. You were a foot and a half taller than AJ, and it was an ugly tie, anyway. Shame on you for not saving my delicate features from spittle.

We were silly tired and giggled all the way home at terrible puns and made very unpastorly remarks about personal space and halitosis. I would head straight to the bedroom and flop on the bed, and you would nestle into your precious recliner and fall soundly to sleep until 2 or 3 in the morning, waking only momentarily and long enough to feel your way to the bed. That would have been what normally happened.

But it wasn't.

The minute you opened the front door and not one creature came bouncing down the hallway, wiggling with excitement, we were suspicious. It was a short trip from the front door to the living room, the floor of which was no longer visible.

It was covered in Pottery Barn couch. The devil's henchman had managed to pull some of the top cushions onto the floor and unstuff them.

Completely unstuff them. There was pillow fiberfill on every square millimeter of floor. There was so much fiberfill, you could barely see the top of the coffee table. We had to wade through it like snowdrifts to get to the couch and figure out how much damage had been done. Two of the cushion covers were close to the couch, one torn to shreds, the other probably salvageable but doomed to look like Raggedy Andy for the rest of its natural life. I was stunned for a moment. I couldn't cry or even utter dismay. I turned, grief stricken, to you. You looked appalled, concerned, but not for me. Dollar signs were flashing across your face, in your eyes, on your lips. Lots and lots of dollar signs.

At that moment, a large pair of black, upright ears poked up above the snowdrifts. For one split second, I could tell you wanted to laugh. Then you looked at me. Murder was in my eyes. Annihilation. Massacre. Dismemberment. A slow death with little left to bury.

You stepped in front of me and put your hand on my shoulder. I think you said something comforting like, "We'll put it back together," or "It will be alright." I don't really remember. All I saw were big black ears that were about to be separated from their owner. You told me later that you had never seen my face that color before. And for a moment, you wondered if you would be able to keep me from pushing you out of the way and killing that dog. You stepped away, turned, and snatched Stitch off the floor. You dumped him out the French doors onto the porch. "Let's get this mess cleaned up," you said. Stitch was standing at the window of the French doors, surveying his handiwork, and looking quite pleased with himself. I could not move; I was frozen stiff in cold fury. Dollar signs were marching across my face, too, but they had more to do with how much of my couch I could cover in Frenchbo hide. Would it be enough to make a whole cushion to replace the ruined one?

By that time, you had brought a couple of those huge, black leaf bags into the house and began scooping giant handfuls of couch stuffing into them. Two bags were not enough. By the time we got it all off the floor, we had five leaf bags of couch stuffing. Pottery Barn couch stuffing. Five-month-old Pottery Barn couch stuffing.

I was sick to my stomach.

After we cleaned up the mess, I headed for the bedroom to get into some pajamas, wishing I liked scotch and that we had some very expensive brand tucked under a counter somewhere. Neither of us drank enough even to call it social drinking, but I was willing to start that night and catch up for all the years lost to abstinence.

As I reached the bedroom door, I saw you at the doors to the back porch, about to open them and let Stitch back into the house.

I'd never felt so calm.

"You let that dog back into this house tonight,
you'll wake up in the morning to a dead dog."
You waited til I was asleep before you let him in.

Letter Number Thirteen

Dear John,

I know, I know, it's not even midnight, but I feel an early bedtime coming on. I have two things on my mind tonight. Well, three.

I made sugar cookies. I wanted to take a picture of them and send them to you, but since that plan wasn't destined for success, I just ate them. Now my stomach hurts. I blame you.

Considering where I believe you to be, this question might sound mildly (or wildly) ridiculous, but do you know what this Sunday is? Yup. Transfiguration Sunday. Since that was my first sermon, what—10 years ago?—and one that I have preached every Transfiguration Sunday after that, I wonder if it ought to be my last sermon before I walk out the church doors.

I remember stepping up to the pulpit in Natchez and gripping it with the ferocity of a soul trying to grab hold of heaven in the middle of a rockslide to Hell. I took my cellphone with me. A visual aid. I glanced out over the congregation, and saw an elderly couple rise and slide quietly from their pew and exit the church. I remember looking straight at you on the first pew (actually, I'm pretty sure I glared at you, full of righteous anger and unshakeable conviction) and wanted to shout, "I TOLD YOU SO!" Instead, I preached. I preached about having a mountaintop experience with the One who would become our Risen Savior. I preached about Cursillo. And love newly discovered. Joy. Change. Confusion. Passionate, idiotic responses to the miraculous. To the Divine. To a call to listen to the Son of God. As it turned out, I was my own congregation; I was preaching to myself. You pointed that out to me numerous times on the long ride home. I remember yelling at both of you. You. God. You didn't yell back. You let God handle that one. So, I am about to preach my 11th Transfiguration Sunday sermon. Not planning to yell at anyone and am leaving my cellphone in the office as per a now long-established habit. The last of my sermons you heard was in 2015. Feel free to drop in this Sunday. You can leave your phone on my desk.

Friday was hard. Much harder than I thought it would be. My first Valentine's Day solo. One V-Day past the extension of things uttered, then forgiven, and plans made. Neither of us had any idea. No clue whatsoever. And here we are. One living and one dead. Or both living. Or both dead. That was how I

felt late Friday. I don't really mind that I'm
still living. I have great peace. And a home.
We have a new granddaughter on the way.
Happiness and joy are still mine to embrace.
To seek out. In life. In grace. In the Divine.

I don't yell at God, anymore. I'm too afraid
of what he might have me doing next.

Love,

Letter Number Fourteen

Dear John,

I'm watching a guilty pleasure, *Lake Placid*, and wouldn't you know it—the producer is John Willett. Now how often is that going to happen?

I'm sick to death of my own cooking, so I jumped in the car to run down to Oriental Palace. Forgot my phone. *I'll just order when I get there*, I thought. Then I'll run to Greer's and pick up some parchment paper and cat treats, run back to Oriental Palace, pick up my honey shrimp, and head to the house. Apparently, the entire western world wanted Chinese food tonight from the Oriental Palace. I was told it would be at least a 45-minute wait. If I spent 45 minutes in Greer's, I wouldn't have enough money left to pay for dinner. So, I thanked the hostess, got back in my car, skipped Greer's altogether, went home, and ate a Spam sandwich. A scorched Spam sandwich, I might add.

As I was leaving the restaurant, though, the hostess asked me if I had a menu at home. I said, "No, I don't." And she handed me one of those little paper menus with 4,000 Chinese dishes on it. I know there will be eye-rolling over this next clause, but on the way back to the house, I opened it and looked over the offerings. My eye b-lined to the family dinner, and I caught myself trying to figure out which of the dishes under Column A you would get and which one I would get from Column B.

It's a good thing our thoughts don't appear in little dialogue bubbles over our heads. I would live in a permanent state of disgrace and embarrassment. Certainly, no one would ever allow me in a pulpit. Of course, I was in the car (yes, reading a menu—big eye roll here; *get it over with*), so probably no one would have noticed my little bubble, but it sort of ticked me off. I wonder how long it will be before I stop doing that. Then, when I think of the reason I need to stop doing that, I feel a little melancholy, because the reason is—you died.

Died is a very tough word to deal with. Not to mention how its context plays out in the real world. There are five definitions of "die" in Webster's. The very last one is "to become indifferent." The example is "to die to worldly things." I suppose that is what you have done, but I resent it. I do. The part of me that is supposed to be happy for you is shrouded in all kinds of spiderweb sticky resentment. I wasn't ready for you to go. Especially not the way you

did. I didn't have three seconds to say goodbye.
I'm grateful as heck that I didn't go flying to
Bay St. Louis to check on you. I'm grateful that
I called Joyce first. I'm grateful that I'm not the
one who found you. It would have been hours
before I would have called for an ambulance.
And you would be all soggy from those tears
that waited until your memorial service to drown
everyone that had the courage to embrace me,
drenched as I was. By the time I had hugged
13 people or so, I thought I'd be out of tears,
but death seems to be a singular exception to
that rule about the percentage of water that can
escape your body before you drop dead (too).

This is not the first letter in which I have
bemoaned this fact. I just thought I might
be further down the road after all this time.
It's automatic. I did the math. I will be 65 in
May. You and I were ostensibly together for
36.5 years. That only leaves 28.5 years, the
duration of which I didn't know you, or you
were gone. More than half of my life, John
Robert. I'm a rational person. I'm not even that
sentimental, anymore. That has been drummed
out of me for a variety of reasons. You helped.

As a rational person, I don't understand why
I occasionally drift into some kind of time warp
in which you are still alive and waiting to be told
which dish you want to order from Column A.
You'd end up ordering sweet and sour shrimp,

no matter what I said. And no matter what I
ordered from Column B, I would want at least a
little bit (two shrimp) of your sweet and sour,
because your food always looked tastier and
more inviting than my food. Why I just didn't
order the same thing you did is a mystery.

Go ahead. Roll your eyes some more
because I bought a new coffee table. You
know I gave up my study when I bought this
house, and, therefore, have nowhere to work.
I've been spread out and bent over our old
coffee table for months now and my back is
tired of it. I found one that has a lift top. It
is way cool. It looks like any ordinary coffee
table, and then ta da! The top lifts and locks
into place like a desk surface. "Why", you
ask, "is this an improvement with all the
junk you spread all over the place?" Well,
Mr. Smarty Pants, it also has storage. I can
sweep everything under the table when I am
ready to stop working and go to bed with both
a clean conscience and a clean workspace.

This is one of those moments when I can't
believe that if I text you, you will not respond.
If I call you, you will not answer. Your number
and your phone have been deactivated for a
long time. If I drove all the way to Bay St.
Louis, I would find some other tenant in your
apartment. I couldn't do that anyway, because

Henri is living with Elizabeth in the front of the house, and I don't think I could take it.

Honestly, I have received more blessings than I can count, yet they are still steeped in feelings of loss and mourning, a diaphanous pall cast over all that has happened. A weary, worn-out teabag of sorrow. Even the joy of owning my very own little farmlet is a bit stained because of your absence. You are not near enough for me to drive you nuts pointing out every little bit of farmlet pleasantry.

I don't suppose you'd be remotely interested in a short vacation from Paradise, would you? We'd be like old friends long separated by time and distance, staying up til all hours of the night talking, promising that next time, it won't be so long before we meet again. I know I'll see you again. If you don't come find me, I'll hunt you down on whatever golf course they let duffers play on in heaven. Whatever is on the table at the Great Banquet, I'll probably want some of what you order. I'm positive sharing at heavenly banquets, while not mandatory, is highly favored.

Does God let you roll your eyes in heaven? Bet not. Must be mighty tough when you're looking at my new coffee table slash desk.

Letter Number Fifteen

Dear John,

The last time we traveled together, we went to see our Colorado Kids. Joey and Johni were a little freaked that they didn't have separate places where we could sleep. When you told Joey we'd be staying in the basement together, I remember a long pause. Eventually, I heard Joey say, "Well, okay. If you're comfortable with that."

It was a great visit. Emi turned four. Johni always went all out on party themes. I think the theme that year was ballerinas. It was a pink tulle blowout. Even a couple of the little boys had on tutus, remember? It was hilarious. And that cake! I thought it was surely the most beautiful cake ever created. White with pink and purple flowers and pearls. Fit for a wedding.

You had already begun to feel not so hot, anymore. I remember how swollen your ankles were when we got off the plane. And though you claimed every day we were married that you were tired, you were actually tired for the duration of that trip. I loved it, though. We had such a great time with the girls and spent probably $300 on take-out dinners. Juliet was just old enough to be wary of strangers, so I don't remember holding her in my arms even once.

Not so you. You were magic with babies. Magic. I'll never understand why. You were huge and hairy and had a black, bristly beard, and a deep voice that was really, really loud most of the time. I always thought had I been a baby and you'd snatched me up off the floor, I'd have screamed in terror and had nightmares for a month. But Joey, Jordan, Emi, Juliet, George, all our children and grandchildren just adored you when they were tiny. I've always said you could wrangle a burp out of a baby rhinoceros. Babies stopped crying when you held them. Your silly baby voice made them giggle. Frankly, I was jealous of your baby-soothing arsenal. Our kids loved my bedtime songs. I take credit for their exposure to Billie Holiday and Nina Simone.

All you had to do was walk down the hallway during my best blues song, and the little traitors would start hollering for a Joey Wowee or Jordy Wardy story. When you spun those tales off the top of your head, Joey and Jordan were rapt. Or giggling wildly. When I sang to them, all they did was fall asleep.

That didn't change with your grandchildren, except that you were too exhausted at the end of the day to climb those stairs with them to tell Emi Wemmy and Juliet Wooliet stories. I think that trip was sort of a wake-up call for me, although, I never in my wildest dreams anticipated that you would up and die on me eight months later. I had no clue whatsoever.

After the wild ones were sent to bed, we'd follow shortly, tromping down the stairs to the basement where Joey and Johni had set up a little "suite" for us. I kept my iPad charged, because that was the year the first Jack Ryan series premiered. You and I would get into our pajamas, jump into that one bed, and load Prime Video. We limited ourselves to one episode per night (discipline I would never have been able to exercise at home). But you always were such a stickler for some weird rules of conduct.

As much as I love our kids and grandchildren, *you* made those trips for me. I had so much more fun when you were there. When it was time to reserve airline tickets for the trip to Denver for Juliet's birthday, you broke it to me that you weren't going to travel anymore. Not even to see our g'babies. At first, I didn't believe you. But your body had taken a severe hit when you came down with Shingles, and I think it was hard for me to recognize and accept that you weren't going to be pulling azaleas straight out of the ground, anymore. When I look back, there were so many clues. And I was oblivious to them all.

Letter Number Sixteen

Dear John,

Why didn't we have a song? Every other couple we'd ever met had a song. Even the ones we knew didn't like each other. Heck, Buckhaults and I had a song, albeit a breakup song, but a song, nonetheless.

Before Jordan and Adam were married, they were seeking just the right song for their first dance after the wedding. I had all kinds of suggestions and found that, apparently, I have an affinity for Paul McCartney love songs. Well, you know I also have a proclivity toward sarcasm, so "When I'm 64" was my first offering. Then "Maybe I'm Amazed" and "No More Lonely Nights."

They chose "It's a Wonderful World." What ...?

I think it's funny. Odd. Neurotic. Even though you've been gone for months, songs keep running through my mind. I am trying to find the perfect one that expresses all the complicated years we were together.

Obviously, you have no say in the song choice, but I consider that your fault. We should have had a song long before you packed me off to Washington as we had already experienced so much in our relationship, both good and bad (remember, you showed up drunk for our second date and insulted my favorite waiter at the Dew Drop Inn). Three roses dangled from my front door the next day, one for each offense, I guess, but I cannot remember what number three was. Maybe drunk counts for two. Why I got in the car with you will forever be a mystery, but since the Dew Drop was only one street away, I must have decided to risk it. I almost called the whole thing off but didn't. Then three weeks later, you dumped me for a Triumph. A car, John Robert. I suppose you decided I might turn out to be more expensive than the note on the Spitfire. I was crushed. Then I was furious. You called me two or three times down the road. Maybe the Spitfire and $1.50 hotdogs laced with insults at the Dew Drop were suddenly within your budgetary restraints.

But a song? Nope. Admittedly, I didn't suggest one, either. You were there and then gone and then there again. Is there a song called "I'm So Confused"? Probably, but neither of us made note of it. I think it's weird. No song indicates a lack of genuine feeling or optimism about the relationship. We lasted 34 years, though, so that sentiment proved untrue. In theory.

Why it is so important to me now is not really a mystery. When I'm feeling particularly maudlin, it would be nice to have some old song from the 70's to howl over. I don't want to cry over you. When I think of you, all I want is for you to come home.

It's eggnog season. At Winn Dixie the other day, I got so excited, I ran over to pick up a couple of half gallons, so we could stir some Kahlua into it and toast our way to Christmas Day. It made me sad.

I put it back.

Our song would have been helpful on the drive home. Singing our song would have been preferable to the wash of misery that rolls over me when I realize the things we will never do together again and that nobody else will ever understand why that's so upsetting. I wouldn't want them to, anyway. Shared memories are only meaningful to the ones who shared them. I don't want to have to explain why this or that was special to me, because it would be something that was special to us. Nope. Not worth it.

I know. Oh, boo hoo. World's smallest violin. Put on your big girl panties.

Blah, blah, blah. Don't want to today. I'd rather howl to our nonexistent song.

Dear John,
    A story instead of a letter:

Moving Out

I got knocked silly once by an errant pitch that slammed into my right shin and crawled right up my face before it glanced off my eye socket to be run down by the second baseman. I tried to stay upright and not cry like a girl. I remember the eternity of those three seconds while I waited for my vision to clear and the world to come back into focus. Even then, I couldn't quite bring myself to move for almost a minute. You shouted out sympathy and encouragement from the bench. "Shake it off, kid!"

On a muggy September morning at our home on St. Charles, I found myself standing at the sink in the bathroom, toothbrush in hand, staring at my reflection in the mirror. I had that same feeling of disorientation and blurred vision. I didn't quite recognize the defeated woman staring back at me. And I couldn't shake it off, anymore. My world came into sharp focus just at the moment I slipped the toothbrush between my lips. "Who the hell **are** you?" It was a serious question. Those dark circles and listless expression were not my own. Surely not. And my eyes looked like stones. Hard and pitiless. Surely those weren't mine, either.

For maybe the fourth or fifth time in my life, I had a profound revelation. I spoke to the stranger in the looking glass. "You can't stay here, anymore." I blinked hard, trying to summon the actual me back into focus. "You can't stay here. As long as you stay, after all that has gone before, you will just disappear little by little. You are giving him (you - I was talking about you, John Robert) tacit permission to continue doing what he's been doing for the last three years."

Two years of counseling had not changed anything for us. You would swear that you were done with it, and then I would round a corner in the house, and you'd be on your iPad, then later, actually on the phone. I couldn't understand how we had gotten to that dark place. The day I found out in August of 2013, we'd had that long, terrible, sit-down talk at the kitchen table. I know you remember that one. I felt gut-punched. You made promises that you wouldn't keep. And for the next couple of years, I believed you over and over again until I just didn't, anymore.

On the way to dinner with friends one night, I asked you for your phone. I hadn't charged mine and didn't think I had enough juice left to make the call to let them know we would be late. You didn't hesitate. You handed me your phone, and no sooner than it passed from your hand to mine, it began to ring. So, I answered. There were about three seconds of silence on the other end, and then a woman asked, very uncertainly, "Is this Johnny's number?" I couldn't think of a single, sensible thing to say, so I just said, "I beg your pardon?" And, whoever that was, she hung up.

You swore. You swore to me that you had no idea who that was or why she asked for you. I was on tenterhooks. My heart had had enough. My mind was screaming at you, calling you a liar, faithless, betrayer ... A couple of dozen adjectives raced through my brain but nothing came out of my mouth. I was utterly speechless. I couldn't argue with you one more time. We ate dinner in silence with one another, talking only to the couple we were eating with, and that silence trailed after our car, a vapor of agony, all the way home from Gulfport to Bay St. Louis. I have no memory whatsoever as to whether I ate a single bite of my dinner.

At home, we separated. You went to your study and turned on the television. I went to the bedroom and got into my pajamas and washed my face. It was a routine we had followed for years. But now there was this new thing, this reality between us that it wasn't just pictures, anymore. Real people were involved, and those people were no longer just you and me. My thoughts as I brushed my teeth were casting about wildly for something to grab hold of, something less hurtful, less overwhelming. Less real. How many? How long? Was I to blame in some way? Was there anything to be done? We had tried talking it out; we'd seen a marriage counselor for a little over two years. We'd stopped seeing him together and had begun to go at different times on different days, never discussing what we each had talked about with Bob.

Eventually, even Bob had thrown up his hands and said he did not know how to help us get past the sticking place. A host of other issues surfaced in my mind as to what it was that drew you in a direction directly opposite me. You chose something, someone, other than me. And on that muggy September morning, the light switched on in my brain that if you couldn't or wouldn't change the way things were, I'd have to.

I didn't pack my little suitcase and walk out the door. You and I sat down again for the umpty-dozenth time to have another talk. We had a little timeshare in a converted Holiday Inn in Destin, and our week was in October. "Let's go to Destin. Let's see if we can figure a way out of this train wreck that has become our marriage." The old college try. Admittedly, I think you wanted to do that as much as I did. I don't think you were one iota happier about the narrowing options for our future than I was. So we went to Destin.

We had eight days to turn things around. Eight days to talk it out. Eight days to salvage our 32 years of marriage. But it only took eight linear feet, while you sat on the couch and I (apparently this was all I did anymore) was standing at the bathroom vanity brushing my teeth. It's a wonder I have a hair's width of enamel left on my teeth. It was a small one-bedroom "condo," and the vanity was open to the kitchen and living area. I could see you from the mirror. Did you know that? Did you realize that I was watching you hammer the last nail in the coffin of our long, long relationship. I think I even asked you that. "Do you realize..." What I realized was, whether you did or didn't, I had to make the next move.

That very moment, as I stared at your reflection from over my shoulder, I decided. I was moving out.

If I loved you at that instant, I couldn't feel it. I couldn't feel a thing.

You didn't, of course, believe I would do it. I'm pretty sure you thought it was all for effect. That I was being melodramatic, overreacting to something you later described to me when we were in the middle of a divorce as merely a form of entertainment.

I was not entertained. I cannot even remember what you said to me, but one night, as I was trying to untangle the infernal mess of all my necklaces hanging on a hook on the closet wall, you made a remark about who was going to take the dogs.

Maybe that wasn't it. Maybe it was about the washer and dryer or the good china or the two rockers on the front porch. I have no specific memory of the reason, but I do remember losing my cool. Not that I'd never lost it before, but I don't ever remember throwing anything at you. I did that night. But it was jewelry, not even good, heavy jewelry. I didn't have the arm strength to heave it all the way across the room, and you would have merely batted it to the side. I wished later I'd picked up the Gibson Girl chair and hurled it at your head. **That** would have gotten your attention. But the twisted chains just fell to the floor, and I snatched them up and crammed them into the suitcase, ready right then and there to leave the house without so much as a by-your-leave or a clean pair of underwear.

I do remember this. You never asked me to stay. You passively helped me load my stuff into a Uhaul trailer and watched me pull out of the driveway and head off to Alabama. You looked forlorn. But you looked forlorn when I asked you to go to a movie, or a play, or anything that didn't involve some sort of ball and a modicum of physical violence, blow-'em-up movies not-withstanding.

Part of me wanted you to run after me, down St. Charles past the railroad tracks, pleading, plaintively, "Come back! Come back!" But we weren't Rose and Jack. You stood stock still in the driveway. And I drove alone and uncertain to Jackson, Alabama, longing only for peace. Longing only for corners in a house that I didn't have to dread turning. Longing for no more discoveries that, try as we might, there was no getting past the place where our misery dwelled as long as we were living in the same house.

I was numb that first night. I'd left with the dining room table and chairs, a chest of drawers, and the guest bed. Less than half the pots and pans and no flatware whatsoever. I slept on the guest bed mattress on the floor. I think in my head I believed I didn't deserve to be in such lofty air as an old, high Jenny Lind bed provided. And for almost three years after that, I wondered about you. How did you sleep that night? What did you think about? Were you sad? Relieved? Lonely? Despairing? What?

You kept the dogs. At least I knew that you were warm and had cuddle buddies. But I can't remember if I drew comfort from that or just resented you all the more. And now, I can't ask you. When I see you again, it won't matter, will it? Everything living thing in the house on St. Charles has died since then. There are no witnesses to what transpired that night. I had even left the cats. No living thing rode with me to Jackson, Alabama, to give me comfort. It was a long night for me. It was probably equally as long for you. I know that now.

But that night, I didn't know anything for sure and certain. Did the dogs even miss me? I knew Stitch was probably luxuriating on my side of the bed, delirious that he didn't have to fight Sam and Karmen and Bill and Cleo for room to stretch out. Did you wake up the next morning with the imprint of the nightstand on your cheek? Our animals were such bed hogs.

I had a whole house to stretch out in. And neither you nor the critters were there for company. I was a stranger in a strange land, and I wondered, not for the only time, why was I the one who moved out? Why didn't I pack *your* little suitcase and just shove *you* out the front door?

Like I said, the next time I see you, it won't matter at all. God surely won't let me smurf you. It doesn't work that way in heaven. Does it?

M

Letter Number Seventeen

Dear John,

You awful, awful man. Every single day, my heart breaks again in new and myriad ways. It is muscle memory to turn to you to ask a question or to get you to fix the lid on the stupid Instapot. And you are ... not ... here.

Early mornings are the worst. I can't tell you how many times I've wakened around 6 and turned over to see if you've gotten up, yet. When I see nothing but empty space and a pillow with no hollow in it, it is like you died all over again.

I don't weep inconsolably. But I often feel tears sliding down my cheeks unbidden. They slip into my ears or drop to my pillow, the one with the hollow in it.

I want to, want to, want to hate you. But my heart won't entertain it. Not even for a minute. We could go weeks without touching one another. I don't know what it is that made sighting you so reassuring. You know me. I used to think about what I might do if I had a harpoon and whether

I would give you a sailor's warning. To be fair.
Since your back was always turned to me.

Elizabeth sent me two pictures of Henri today.
He looks like a fat, happy little sausage. I hope
he doesn't remember us. I know nothing about
whether dogs have long-term memories, but I do.
My last memory of Henri is seeing him through
the fence at your apartment, all wiggly and
wanting me to come pick him up. I turned
my back on him and drove away in your truck.
I broke my own heart that day. It still hurts.
A lot.

Where is that tough teacher-hide I used to
have? Where is that tough "you can't hurt me,
anymore" shield I had for so many years? Why
am I crying in the middle of the day? You went
home to Jesus. Why couldn't you take my
memories with you?

I am so tired. Honestly, I don't think you're
an awful, awful man. Not all the time.

Love/not love,

Letter Number Eighteen

Dear John,

Calling all grandfathers. Your children are still having children. Please return to the delivery waiting room, Mr. Willett. You now have six grandchildren. I'm a little jealous, as I can only officially claim four of them, but I'm sending pajamas in your memory to the all the babies at Christmas. We make such idiots out of ourselves at Christmas here. I cannot begin to imagine what it looks like from your perspective now. My 9-foot tree wouldn't merit a passing glance in your neighborhood. I hope they aren't letting you hang lights. Not that you were bad at it. You always got them up. They always looked good. I never knew how you survived the process. How can a human six-and-a-half-foot body lean at a 90-degree angle from the top of a ladder for thirty minutes at a stretch for ... one ... dangling ... bulb at a time.

Yikes.

You were the most impossible man. Does God smirk every time I say that? Have you

asked Him? Never mind. You probably think
He takes your scorecard at face value.

Letter Number Nineteen

Dear John,

You can't forget how to breathe. You can forget to breathe for a few seconds but then autonomic responses kick in. It might feel like you have forgotten to breathe forever. But you can't do it. Here's something to think about. You can certainly forget to enjoy it. You can start to breathe in jerky, little unsatisfying clutches of breath that keep your body moving but not much else. You can live your life that way, too. Surfacing occasionally for a snatch of abbreviated air to see what is going on around you and then submerging again into a murky half-life, where barely enough gets done to quantify it as living.

I think I kept moving. In most ways, I felt I had to. We had to arrange your cremation. We had to pick up your ashes. We had to have a memorial. We had to clean out your apartment. We had to figure out where to put all that stuff. Most of it ended up in my carport and followed me, bedraggled and sad, to my new home. More than half of it is still out there. Boxes piled up like mournful reminders of tasks left undone.

I have adjusted. I have found joy in my start-all-over-again Life #47. I am surrounded by cows, donkeys, horses, and of course, my own three chickens. I enjoy this more than I can say, and I'm not even sure why. I think I'm finally where I'm supposed to be. The horses eat apples and carrots out of my hand. The sweet donkeys will roll over on their backs, begging for a belly rub and anything the horses deign not to eat.

Lady lives with me now. I remember when we got her for Jordan ten years ago.

I like the memory of when we brought her home to Pass Christian before we took her up to Jackson. Our dogs went nuts. Lady freaked out. You got covered in excrement and urine because Lady was so scared. I always chose the most inappropriate times to break into raucous laughter. But your face. Oh, my word.

The sun shines. The rain falls. The moon rises in various shapes, sizes, and occasionally lovely colors. I have porch swings front and back. Breezes. Kind neighbors. Church. The bills are paid. All the appliances work. Nothing to complain about. Peaceful more often than not. The desire to tell you this, to show you this, remains constant. These are the only times a tiny hollow note peals into my heart. Even that's not so bad anymore. It brings a

brief melancholy with it—short-lived and it no
longer lingers throughout the remaining day.

I can see colors now. The pall has been lifted.
Breathing brings pleasure. It brings life.

Every year around our birthdays, I determine
it is time to retire. That intent passes. You
can't feed horses and chase chickens 24/7.
God still has work for me to do. I can live
with that. And without you, I suppose.

Letter Number Twenty

Dear John,

Tomorrow, I won't want to write you any letters, so I'm doing it tonight. Tomorrow it will be one year. Tomorrow your children will mourn. Tomorrow I will mourn. Not that we haven't done that over the past 12 months. And even though I've never really bought into Elisabeth Kubler Ross's take on the stages of death and dying, I'm having to reassess my opinion. I don't think the stages of grief are that tightly organized. I think that most of them happen out of order and some more than once. But they do happen.

I have lived alone for 5 years now. I have no problem with that. The problem I do have is having no sounding board, no editor, no one who shares the greatest part of the history of my life. I have a problem with the fact that I still go into Dillard's where a shirt catches my eye and I think to myself, *John would look good in that color.* You were always so color brave when it came to wearing hues you wouldn't have picked in a zillion years because I thought you looked good in pink, coral, lavender. I could not get you out of those Oxford shirts, though. And I still find myself bemused that, as frugal (read cheap) as you were, when you bought shoes, you wanted the $150 kind. Couldn't begrudge you that. You wore t-shirts from Walmart.

On February 14, a great day to do it, you said things to me I never in my life thought I would hear. On the last trip to see Bob, when you dropped me off at my house, you said what you always said, "I love you, kid." My response for years had been, "I know." That day was different. I had not said what I said for many years. I said, "I love you, too." And I am so grateful for that. That was Thursday and on Sunday you were gone. Did you know? Were all the things we talked about on those two days your way of saying goodbye?

When I got there on Monday, I was comforted and devastated, at the same time, that your shoes were polished and on the bed. Your suit was hanging on the door frame, and you had a pair of undies and a clean t-shirt rolled up in the bathroom on the shelf above the toilet. You were still in your pajamas, but you were getting ready to go preach at Gautier. I know that most of your life, for our whole 35 years together, and beyond that, you wanted to be in ministry. Seminary didn't work out for you. You had to go home. I know that left a little fissure in your heart that never quite healed until Old Town said, "We want you to serve here." You were a decent preacher straight out of the gate. I was awful for five solid years. Really, really awful. But you encouraged me, anyway, even though I know you knew that I didn't want to be there, that my sermons weren't up to snuff, and that I wanted to give up about 500 times because of Al and Judy. There is no chance that I would have stayed over 5 years otherwise. Had I quit, I wouldn't be at First Prez. This church has been nothing but a gift. I have learned not to give up so easily. I have learned to love people even when they criticize. I have learned that criticism could inform my ministry and guide me, as I learned what needed to be done.

I am here for the long run, I guess. I don't want to tell God what I am going to do. I learned my lesson on that trip home from Natchez. Before I committed. Before I thought it was even possible. Before I shouted at you, "If God wants me to go into ministry, He's going to have to tell me Himself."

I look back at that moment, both appalled and amazed. That December, Old Town called us to come. And by April, they wanted us to stay. More than one person told me a husband and wife co-pastorship would not work. I was always surprised that no matter what happened in our lives outside the church, we never had a hard time working together. I wish we had both had a little more courage at home, but we learned to be courageous at church and to seek out ministry that extended beyond the doors of the Old Town sanctuary. Ministry was a good choice for both of us and a blessing that cannot be measured, coming so late in life.

I think this will be my last letter, John. I can't say it's time to move on. I believe grief and a deep sense of melancholy will be part of my heart and mind for the rest of my life. But these letters are hard to write; they remind me of what I will no longer have from here on out. But I will not forget.

During the last couple of years, I think my favorite thing was that you were willing to read all those chapters of my memoir, even when some of it was painful for you. And truly, truly, truly—

We had the best text life ever.

Postlude One

Dear John,

This won't be part of a mournful, protracted goodbye, but I think you need to know where I am and what I am doing today. I am, at long last, under the Tuscan sun, and it is GLORIOUS.

I am sitting on a small, covered patio outside an old, converted stone house about 15 miles outside of San Gimignano. (I'm sure I just massacred the town's name but have no internet this instant to look up the proper spelling). Even though Weather Channel predicted nothing but rain and overcast skies for most of our visit to Italy, I am bathed in brilliant sunlight at this moment. The temperature is chilly but pleasant.

There are three assorted cats at my feet and several more scattered across the patios and porches that surround the farmhouse. Currently, there are two on the table with me, one purring like a freight train and casually strolling across my keyboard. I'm using the delete key a lot.

I really need you to see what I am seeing. So, pay attention.

In front of me, there are the gentle undulating hills I have dreamed about all my life. Each hill is peppered with olive groves. There is a pergola of some sort directly to my left that is covered by an ancient grape vine, still barren, but promising to flourish at any moment. A peach tree is in full bloom, its dark grey trunk twisted and swathed in fierce, white flowers.

A low border of hedges is hemmed in with lichen-covered rocks built up three deep. Roses, lilies, and oleanders have just begun to pop through the soil. No blooms, yet, but you can see they are coming soon. To my right is an orange tree, trimmed up from the bottom, so that the leaves and branches form a sort of canopy. I can't see the top, but the bottom is draped in fat orange teardrops so beautiful I want to run over and pick one and squeeze its juices into a cup. I won't do it, though. It is too lovely a sight to disturb on this breezy Tuscan morning.

Beyond the hedge, one hill rolls into another. The hosts are organic gardeners. I can see fennel, lettuce, and some plants I can't identify growing not fifteen yards away from my little table tiled in blue and yellow, arranged in sunburst patterns. Two farmhands are working the compost pile. Rows of clay pots are stacked against the house and around our patio, filled with fiery red blossoms. Others are situated near my feet, overflowing with some kind of succulent

I don't recognize. Old wine barrels bear all manner of blooms. The pot nearest me is joined to the frame of our patio cover with a glistening spider's web. A couple of melancholy insects are trapped in its thick silk, a spider's brunch.

Kimber has joined me with another cup of hot tea, so I'll sign off for now and write more later.

The Italian cat is back, anyway, typing lots of symbols that I'm convinced are Italian curse words. Delete. Delete. Delete.

Caio,

Postlude Two

Dear John,

Why did you not tell me about Venice?? Never mind. Too much foreknowledge would have spoiled it a little, but oh my. I feel as though I've died and gone to, well, *Italy*. This place is old world in the way I pictured it during art history class at Millsaps. Thank you, Miss Millsaps, for the best slice of education I ever received. Being able to identify the art and architecture was topped only by being able to stump the Switzaly Gals on naming the different types of columns surrounding the Piazza San Marco, which is where I sat spellbound for several hours drinking cappuccino, while a pigeon I named Clyde hopped all over my shoulders, refusing to leave after I hand fed him one cookie crumb, hoping to pester me out of another one. You know Dad would have completely freaked. But it's Italy. And I'm learning the lingo, if not the actual language, although I've got "Dove' il bagno" down pat.

Euros are a little irksome because any
denomination less than five means coins—thick,
heavy coins which won't fit into my wallet.
That means loose change rattling around the
bottom of my purse. When I walk, I sound like
Santa Claus. And the only thing that costs
one euro in Venice (or elsewhere in Italy) is
a refrigerator magnet. I hope everybody likes
fridge magnet replicas of gondolas because
that's what I'm bringing home. But I promise,
if I have to live on cheese and crackers until
I'm back stateside, it will be worth it to just
absorb the colorful buildings, the surprisingly
green, unsmelly waters of the canals, the
historically narrow cobblestone streets, the
breathtaking cathedrals, and the myriad
bridges that festoon the city's wider canals.

The restaurants and the food are phenomenal.
Seriously. I'm a little concerned about my
budget going bust due to the extravagantly
rich (in euros and calories) fare Venice
has to offer. Not to mention a closet fear of
becoming so wide I'll have to navigate the
city turned sideways to squeeze through the
lovely, narrow alleyways that connect the big
piazzas one to the other, each with endless
options of gelato and refrigerator magnets.

Gondolas are a real thing. Maybe a little
hokey in a very touristy sort of way but still
charming enough to shell out 80 euros to let

a gondolier glide you through the city paying you outrageously insincere compliments and telling silly jokes. I want to buy a little black and white striped gondolier tee, but the girls have ridiculed me mercilessly about doing so. All that means is that I'll have to be crafty about the purchase and hide it somewhere in my battered, duct-taped suitcase only to consign it to the sleeping tee drawer along with our James Taylor shirts from February 2019. I brought James with me. You know why.

It could be that I don't understand the concept of jet lag, but after more than a week, while I'm not tired, I still have my days and nights turned around. You'd better be glad you're not allowed to cart your iPhone around your current residence, or I'd be blowing that sucker up at all hours. I do wish we could have shared this. It feels like a place we should have seen together. It's so, so charming in all the best pastel pink and orange ways.

Caio,

Postlude Three

Dear John,

   We arrived in Domossodola at dusk. The
mountains were barely discernible against the
dark sky. Flickering lights ascended the side
of the rocky juts not quite reaching the top.
Homes and businesses, churches and chimneys
promised a better view in the morning. We were
late getting in and other than an introduction
to our hosts and a cursory glance around the
bed and breakfast everyone piled into bed to
rest after the rush to the train, a four-hour
ride that whooshed by towns and lakes and
farmland, then a hair-raising taxi ride up and
down perilously (or so it seemed) steep curves
on streets more narrow than in Venice.

   I woke up early (for me) because I couldn't
wait to see if the landscape outside matched the
pictures posted on the Airbnb site. Oh my. We're
in the burg where Charlie lived when he drew
the golden ticket to the chocolate factory. We're
up in the mountains. I don't know how high, but
high enough for there to be three snow-covered

peaks right outside the window. The houses
are tiled in grey stone shingles, each with a
fireplace peeking above the roof. Most of the
houses are a creamy white-to-pale yellow with
a few that look as though they have never been
painted. Those houses are worn and ancient
looking but seem almost more appropriate to
the setting than the painted ones. I can see
spruce and fir, and, below our balcony, what
looks like a ginormous Christmas tree. There
are indications of spring: yellow flowers and
fruit trees with new blooms, a bush with melon-
colored blossoms. I have no idea what it is.

The narrow streets rush to the hilltops
and tumble into the valleys, and—this is my
favorite part so far—they are all lined with
stone fences that start low at the streets
and rise up, stone upon stone, to the walls of
the houses. Cars hide behind them in yards
neatly hemmed in by the stone hedges. I
can't see a single garage from our window.

It's hard to gauge distance because of the
hilly terrain, but I'm looking at a tall church
spire with four arched windows at the top.
There is a bell visible on the two sides I can
see. It's already rung once to welcome in
the day. I can see the ever-present pigeons
perched on the bell tower, which is also the
proprietor of a clock that displays an hour
nowhere near the actual time of day.

As far as I can tell, we are in a little
valley surrounded by peaks to the east,
west, and south. There are no windows to
the north. I'll have to check that out later.

Our hosts are Luigi and Louisa. They live
on floor zero. We are on the first floor, and
their daughter and two nieces live on the floor
above us. Louisa told us last night that the
children were already in bed but that we would
hear them pattering around in the morning.
She was right. We share a common hall, and
someone left the house a few minutes ago, but
I couldn't see who. Luigi and Louisa are very
welcoming. We stepped into a house that's been
here since the 1600's. Wine and cheese were
in the kitchen. The makings for tea and coffee
in the cupboard. We were pleased that the only
two bedrooms in the apartment were huge
and easily accommodated us all. As usual, the
bathrooms are fabulous. The walls are stone
and stucco. There are massive beams supporting
the ceilings and rustic furniture dotting the
room. Except for this chair. It's one of those
chairs with a remote control that rises to help
you get up and lifts the footrest automatically.
It seems oddly out of place, but here I sit, my
feet on the footrest, with a cup of tea, gazing
at this demi-town right on the Swiss border.

I suspect there will no crowds bustling
in the streets here. I'll be on the lookout

for men in lederhosen and hats with little feathers poking from the brim. Right now, I am looking at a man with a huge backpack and two ski poles, trudging up the incline of a tiny street. He's wearing ski pants. I can't tell if he's walking so slowly because of age, infirmity, or the challenge of the uphill climb.

I have no idea what we are going to do today. It's a down day. We're planning what we will do the next few days. I will also be on the hunt for a chocolatier when we actually cross the Swiss border. You know what that means. I will buy chocolates to bring home as gifts, and half of them will be gone before I am on the plane in Milan headed for home.

I know you've been to this part of the world. I wonder if you looked out a similar window in amazement at God's incredible landscapes rising up as layers of rock and evergreens, topped with snow, with tiny villages tucked in a hollow beneath them. As much as I adored Venice, this is a new place with new pleasures to offer, and I am excited to be here. It's easy to see that this will be a completely different kind of journey. I'm hoping to practice my rusty German in a few of the towns we will be visiting. Most people here speak French. Thus, I am doomed to communicate with hand signals. Italian is so much easier. We'll see about the German. I can hear it so clear and crisp in my head but will probably sound like Sylvester Stallone trying to pronounce "dawg" in that movie with Dolly Parton.

Ooh, an all-black bird just streaked past my window. And there's a sheep dog! Where the heck are the sheep?

Still Caio at this point.,

Epilogue

John's ashes are in a rosewood box way up on top of an antique secretary in my living room. They're not going anywhere until I do. We'll be buried in the same plot with a single headstone. He asked me many years ago to sprinkle his ashes into the 9th hole at the Pascagoula Country Club. I took the liberty of assuming that to be a joke. We did talk seriously about scattering our ashes, but as members of our families have died, I now recognize the value of having a place for other friends and family to come and read our names on a headstone. To remember and reflect on our lives. To reflect on their own mortality. To appreciate the brevity of life in this world and to be moved to fully immerse themselves in each hour God has granted.

I did not expect John to die at 71. I did not expect to see my 66th year. I am not in charge, however. This knowledge has grown sweeter with each passing day, because my job is to make the most of this one and let God take care of tomorrow.

In Matthew 6:24, Jesus tells His followers, "Therefore do not be anxious about tomorrow, for tomorrow will be anxious for itself. Sufficient for the day is its own trouble." (English Standard Version translation)

While today may have enough trouble of its own, it also has its pleasures: discoveries, sweet moments, grass under bare feet, and perhaps donkeys begging for a belly rub. Your day may be all about the beach, or a book, or your children, or your grandchildren. Your loss does not lodge a period at the end of this day. Believe in redemption. Believe in resurrection. Hold fast to hope. Hold fast to God. Hold a friend's hand. Remember fondly. Allow your grief to make its own way through your heart, through your life. Grief is not itself a death knell. Don't enshrine the loved one you've lost. Let them wander through the chambers of your heart freely. All the good shared when they lived here does not dissipate at death. Those memories are just as real, just as valuable, and just as viable today as they were the moment they occurred.

God is love. His love never fails. 1 Corinthians 13:8 reminds us of that.

Peace be unto you.

Author's Notes

Even though four years have passed since John's death, I catch myself wondering if he knows where I've placed the so-and-so, which he probably would and tell me, were he still within hearing range. It no longer brings me to tears. It's more like a trip to the mailbox on a federal holiday; I come away empty-handed but not awash in sorrow. The mailbox is still an old friend I like to visit.

If the truth be told, I still write down snippets of my thoughts about our lives together and now apart. Little poems. Silly hand drawn heart bouquets. I occasionally take myself out to dinner at a favorite restaurant and toast his memory or the significance of a date we once celebrated together — then tape the receipt to the place where I keep such things. I frequently find myself cheered these days when I let those memories slip into the light for a moment or two.

I'm hopeless at journaling, but I do like to have a place where I can corral all my ramblings about our life together in one spot, so I can look back over moments in that journey and see how I feel now compared to then and so on.

Following these notes, you will find a few pages where you can record your own thoughts or drawings or place pressed flowers — whatever suits you. Use your imagination. Be authentic. Tell your loved one how you really feel! You'll be surprised at how this helps you wrap your mind around your heart's great yearning. Since I believe in life after death in the presence of a loving God, I imagine what it will be like to sit at table with the Lord and John to hear the **real** truth about John's golf scores.

May your blessings abound! "Weeping may endure for a night, but joy comes in the morning." (Psalm 30:5)

"No, in all these things we are more than conquerors through him who loved us. For I am convinced that neither death nor life, neither angels nor demons, neither the present nor the future, nor any powers, neither height nor depth, nor anything else in all creation, will be able to separate us from the love of God that is in Christ Jesus our Lord."

—Romans 8:37 KJV

Notes

_____
_____
_____
_____
_____
_____
_____
_____
_____
_____
_____
_____
_____
_____
_____
_____
_____
_____
_____
_____
_____
_____
_____
_____
_____
_____
_____

Notes

_____
_____
_____
_____
_____
_____
_____
_____
_____
_____
_____
_____
_____
_____
_____
_____
_____
_____
_____
_____
_____
_____
_____
_____
_____

Notes

_____

_____

_____

_____

_____

_____

_____

_____

_____

_____

_____

_____

_____

_____

_____

_____

_____

_____

_____

_____

_____

_____

_____

_____

_____

_____

_____

_____

_____

Notes

_____
_____
_____
_____
_____
_____
_____
_____
_____
_____
_____
_____
_____
_____
_____
_____
_____
_____
_____
_____
_____
_____
_____
_____
_____

Notes

_____

_____

_____

_____

_____

_____

_____

_____

_____

_____

_____

_____

_____

_____

_____

_____

_____

_____

_____

_____

_____

_____

_____

_____

_____

_____

_____

_____

Notes

_____
_____
_____
_____
_____
_____
_____
_____
_____
_____
_____
_____
_____
_____
_____
_____
_____
_____
_____
_____
_____
_____
_____
_____
_____
_____

Notes

Notes

_____
_____
_____
_____
_____
_____
_____
_____
_____
_____
_____
_____
_____
_____
_____
_____
_____
_____
_____
_____
_____
_____
_____
_____

Notes

Milton Keynes UK
Ingram Content Group UK Ltd.
UKHW010726200923
429044UK00004B/231

9 798218 958695